KT-548-303

THE
COOK'S
FRIEND

THE COOK'S FRIEND

Copyright © Summersdale Publishers Ltd, 2011

With research by Stephen Brownlee, Chris Humphrey and Paul Morriss.

Illustrations by Kath Walker.

All rights reserved.

No part of this book may be reproduced by any means, nor transmitted, nor translated into a machine language, without the written permission of the publishers.

Condition of Sale
This book is sold subject to the condition that it shall not, by way of trade or otherwise, be lent, re-sold, hired out or otherwise circulated in any form of binding or cover other than that in which it is published and without a similar condition including this condition being imposed on the subsequent publisher.

Summersdale Publishers Ltd
46 West Street
Chichester
West Sussex
PO19 1RP
UK

www.summersdale.com

Printed and bound by CPI Group (UK) Ltd, Croydon, CR0 4YY

ISBN: 978-1-84953-190-0

Substantial discounts on bulk quantities of Summersdale books are available to corporations, professional associations and other organisations. For details telephone Summersdale Publishers by telephone (+44-1243-771107), fax (+44-1243-786300) or email (nicky@summersdale.com).

THE
COOK'S
FRIEND

A MISCELLANY OF
WIT AND WISDOM

ILLUSTRATIONS BY KATH WALKER

ALASTAIR WILLIAMS

summersdale

Contents

INTRODUCTION

There is no love sincerer than the love of food.

GEORGE BERNARD SHAW

Many people's warmest childhood memories revolve around food. Whether it's a Sunday roast with all the trimmings, a knickerbocker glory, or, if you're Proust, a freshly baked Madeleine, the flavours and aromas of food take us back to the innocent pleasure of childhood.

What better way is there to recreate that untroubled state of mind than donning an apron and making a meal? The pleasingly practical tasks of chopping, stirring and frying lift our thoughts far from the daily grind and allow us to focus on the moment and unleash our creativity. From those who will whip up a batch of cakes on a wet afternoon to the extravagant home chefs creating luxurious banquets for their friends and families, cooking is accessible for everyone and for many of us it's the pleasure we give as much as the pleasure we receive that makes the effort worthwhile.

Food's importance in life cannot be overstated. Not only do we need it to survive, but what we eat defines us, as French gastronomist Jean Anthelme Brillat-Savarin stated in his 1825 book *The Physiology of Taste*: 'Tell me what you eat and I will tell you what you are.'

Despite all the soufflés that don't rise, the joints that get burnt, and the snooty waiters we encounter, few pleasures on earth can compete with the pride of putting together the perfect dish, or the delight of eating it.

This miscellany, for anyone who's ever thought about wielding anything from a spatula to a carving knife – or even just a menu – contains a smorgasbord of interesting trivia, a dessert trolley-full of practical tips, and a Jeroboam of the best quotes and poems on what can only be described as 'Food, glorious food!'

One cannot think well, love well, sleep well, if one has not dined well.

VIRGINIA WOOLF

Some people have a foolish way of not minding, or pretending not to mind, what they eat. For my part, I mind my belly very studiously, and very carefully; for I look upon it, that he who does not mind his belly will hardly mind anything else.

JAMES BOSWELL, *THE LIFE OF SAMUEL JOHNSON*

If all else fails, just smile and say you like the food.

JOHN BARLOW, *EVERYTHING BUT THE SQUEAL*

How We Eat

*The art of dining well is no slight art,
the pleasure not a slight pleasure.*

MICHEL DE MONTAIGNE

THE STORIES BEHIND THE MEALS WE EAT

Morning meal – breakfast

Breakfast is the first meal of the day, which breaks the fast since the last meal was taken the evening before. In medieval times, the Church discouraged the taking of breakfast, as it was considered breaking the overnight fast too soon. By the fifteenth century, however, breakfast had become more socially acceptable.

The wedding breakfast is the symbolic first meal eaten after a wedding. Unlike breakfast as it is generally understood, it is not necessarily in the morning. One theory is that before the Protestant Reformation, weddings were held at Mass, and people would fast before Mass, the wedding breakfast being when the married couple broke their fast. Another says that before 1887 the law stipulated weddings should be conducted before noon.

*He that but looketh on a plate of
ham and eggs to lust after it hath
already committed breakfast
with it in his heart.*

C. S. LEWIS

Midday meal – dinner or lunch?

This meal was originally called dinner, from the Old French *disner*, which itself comes from the vulgar Latin *disjejunare*, meaning to break one's fast – this being the first meal of the day before breakfast became common. It was also the main meal of the day. From the mid seventeenth century, this meal became smaller and was known as lunch, taken from a medieval German word for a meal inserted between more substantial meals.

Evening meal – supper, tea or dinner?

When two meals a day was the accepted norm, this meal was known as supper and was a lighter meal to tide one over until dinner the next day. The word is related to the Old French *souper* or *super* and the German word *suppe*, referring to soup. This meal may also be known as tea, or high tea, to differentiate it from low tea (or cream tea), as high tea is eaten at a dinner table and low tea from coffee tables. As work patterns shifted, the main meal of the day moved to evening, taking the word dinner with it.

On rainy days alone I dine
Upon a chick and pint of wine.
On rainy days I dine alone,
And pick my chicken to the bone;
But this my servants much enrages,
No scraps remain to save board-wages.
In weather fine I nothing spend,
But often spunge upon a friend;
Yet, where he's not so rich as I,
I pay my club, and so good b'ye.

JONATHAN SWIFT, 'THE DEAN'S MANNER OF LIVING'

Are You Being Served?

Service à la française refers to the custom favoured in Britain until the early nineteenth century of all the dishes of a meal being brought to the table at once. Though an impressive spectacle, it was often impractical as the food could not be eaten at its peak, with the food cooling (or heating up) towards room temperature. In some countries such as Japan, the whole meal is still served together as one big course, generally with no dessert other than hot tea.

Service à la russe, where the meal is served in a sequence of courses, was introduced to France in the early nineteenth century by Russian ambassador Alexander Kurakin and later caught on in England. When this system was first adopted by the French, meals were made up of over a dozen courses, including a shellfish course, a soup course, three sweet courses, a cheese course, a fish course, a roast course and a number of vegetable courses. A simpler variation of *service à la russe* is used in most restaurants in Britain today.

In Italy, a traditional meal includes the *aperitivo* (equivalent to the French *aperitif*), a cold starter, a hot starter, the main course and side dishes, dessert, fruit, another drink and coffee. In Sweden, the *smorgasbord* began in the fourteenth century as the *brännvinsbord*, a buffet-style starter sometimes served up to five hours before a main meal. In the seventeenth century this method of serving became popular for the main course, and included both hot and cold dishes.

Another peculiarity of this country is the absence of napkins, even in the homes of the wealthy. Napkins, as a rule, are never used and one has to wipe one's mouth on the tablecloth, which in consequence suffers in appearance.

BARON LOUIS DE CLOSEN ON AMERICAN EATING HABITS (1780)

Never allow butter, soup or other food to remain on your whiskers. Use the napkin frequently.

THOMAS E. HILL, *HILL'S MANUAL OF SOCIAL AND BUSINESS FORMS: ETIQUETTE OF THE TABLE*

NAPKINS

Napkins have been around since the Spartans used dough to make *apomagdalies* to wipe their hands on. They have subsequently appeared throughout history all over the world in various shapes and sizes and have masqueraded under different names: *sudaria*, *mappae*, handkerchief, *couche*, *portpayne*, serviette and diaper to name but some. At a dinner party, your guests would certainly expect to see a napkin at their place, but what type? Whatever your preference, an intricate swan or a simple fold, a clean napkin is a must. The following are some classic designs:

Candle

Fan

Lily

Shell

Butterfly

Lady's Slipper

The Bishop's Hat (Mitre)

The Standing Fan

Pyramid

The Diamond

Swan

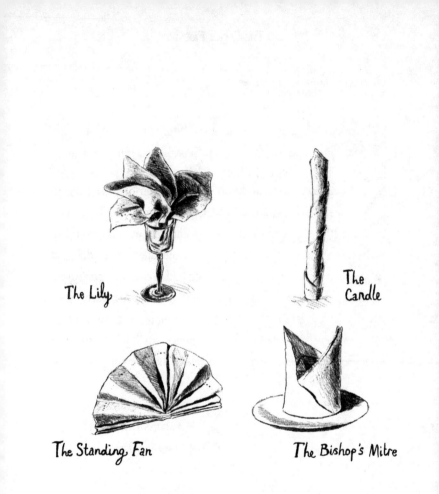

The Lily

The Candle

The Standing Fan

The Bishop's Mitre

Pop-up Restaurants

Though they only entered British culture in the last ten years, pop-up restaurants or supper clubs have been going much longer in the US and Cuba (where they are known as *paladares*). A pop-up restaurant can be created wherever there is space, be it your living room, garden or roof terrace. You open your home as a restaurant and invite guests to dine, asking for a nominal donation – partly to avoid the legal problems associated with charging a fee, and partly to keep the event friendly and social. If you have some space, some time and some cooking talent, why not try it yourself?

Music with dinner is an insult both to the cook and the violinist.

G. K. Chesterton

Say it with Eggs –
Holding a Dinner Party

Impress your friends with a dinner party and they'll think you are a *good egg* but if it all goes wrong you could end up with *egg on your face*. Hosting a good party may take a lot of money and effort but you *can't make an omelette without breaking eggs*. Devote the same amount of attention to each course; you don't want *all your eggs in one basket*. The right atmosphere is important so *egg them on* for a drink or two; you don't want the guests *walking on eggshells*. After the meal clean all the pots and pans yourself, you don't want to seem like a *rotten egg*.

MEALS TO GO

Cornish pasty – A pastry case filled with beef, swede, potato and onion, and crimped closed. The thick crimped edge may have been very useful for Cornish miners as it would allow them to eat the pasty with their hands and then throw the crust away, avoiding touching their food or mouth with their dirty fingers.

Bedfordshire clanger – Similar to the Cornish pasty, the Bedfordshire clanger is made from suet pastry and has one end filled with meat and one with jam. It was originally made as a complete meal for farm labourers to eat whilst out in the fields.

Bento – The word bento originates from a Japanese slang term for 'convenience', and describes a Japanese meal-in-a-box. The origins can be traced back nearly a thousand years, to hoshi-ii, cooked and dried rice that was stored in small bags. Bento today consists of a whole meal of rice with fish or meat and a number of cooked or pickled vegetables. The design of bento dishes has become part of Japanese culture, with kyaraben being bento made to look like a character from a comic book video game character, and oekakiben being decorated to look like a person, animal, building or landscape. Contests are often held.

Tiffin and dabbawalas – The word tiffin comes from an obsolete English word, tiffing, meaning to take a small sip. It was adopted into Indian English and now, particularly in Mumbai, refers to a hot, packed lunch. Tiffins are often delivered by a dabbawala, a type of bicycle courier who solely deals with the collection of tiffins from homes and delivery to the work place. The tiffin containers or dabbas themselves are tiered lunch boxes, usually made from steel, that can keep food warm for at least two hours.

LUNCHTIME ATOP A SKYSCRAPER

During the construction of the centrepiece skyscraper of New York's Rockefeller Center, the immense height of the building meant workers did not have time to return to ground level to eat their lunch. The photographic director of the building, Charles Clyde Ebbets, documented this with his world famous photograph, *Lunchtime atop a Skyscraper*. It depicts seven construction workers sitting along a girder on the second highest story of the seventy-storey building, dangling their feet over the streets hundreds of feet below.

Extreme Dining

Dangling from a crane – For those who want fine dining and an adrenaline rush all in one sitting, a table is suspended from a crane up to 50 metres in the air, and diners are strapped into chairs for safety. Dinner in the Sky is based in Belgium but can be transported anywhere.

In the dark – Restaurants such as Dans Le Noir in London offer a pitch black dining environment. The idea is to remove the customer's sense of sight, so you focus more on your senses of taste and smell. Blind waiters are often employed as the darkness does not affect their ability to work.

Undersea – Maldives restaurant Ithaa, meaning 'pearl', is 5 metres below sea level, and has a transparent acrylic roof giving patrons a panoramic view. The restaurant seats only fourteen people and its expected lifespan is twenty years.

Volcano barbecue – The El Diablo Restaurant in Lanzarote, Spain, was built on top of an active volcano, and food is cooked using the heat from the volcano on a grill over a thermal vent.

All mine – The salt mine in Wieliczka, Poland, produced salt for 700 years from the thirteenth century. Tourists can eat at the Miners' Tavern, located 125 metres underground.

Sweets for My Sweet

All you need is love. But a little chocolate now and then doesn't hurt.

CHARLES M. SCHULZ

Naughty But Nice – Favourite Biscuits

Digestive biscuit – When originally created in the late 1800s, the high sodium bicarbonate content in the sweetmeal biscuit was thought to have an antacid effect and aid digestion.

Bath Oliver – Invented by Dr William Oliver of Bath around 1750, the recipe for this hard, savoury biscuit was left in his will to his coachman, Atkins, who used it to set up a business and became rich.

Bourbon – Made up of chocolate fondant sandwiched between two dark chocolate biscuits, and possibly named for the House of Bourbon, the former royal house of France, this biscuit has inspired much debate on the best way to eat it.

Nice – A coconut flavoured biscuit with the word NICE imprinted on it, produced for over a hundred years. Pronunciation and derivation is disputed: originally made in the French city of Nice, or simply 'naughty but nice'?

Garibaldi – Currants squashed between two biscuits, named for General Giuseppe Garibaldi of Italy, who visited Tynemouth in England in 1854, seven years before the manufacture of the first Garibaldi biscuit.

Seize the moment. Remember all those women on the Titanic who waved off the dessert cart.

ERMA BOMBECK

I want to have a good body, but not as much as I want dessert.

JASON LOVE

Without ice cream, there would
be darkness and chaos.

DON KARDONG

CLASSIC BRITISH PUDDINGS

Roly-poly jam pudding – Also known as jam roly-poly, a flat suet pudding spread with jam and rolled in a similar way to a Swiss roll. A recipe for this dessert is included in Mrs Beeton's cookbook.

Spotted dick – A suet pudding containing dried fruit and cooked by steaming. The recipe was first seen in print in 1850, in Alexis Soyer's *The Modern Housewife of Menagere*. It is called 'spotted' because of the fruit in it, and the 'dick' may be from the German word for thick, or a corruption of the last syllable of pudding, or a corruption of the word dough.

Eton mess – Originating and deriving its name from Eton College near Windsor, this dessert consists of fresh fruit (nearly always strawberries), broken meringue pieces and cream. The word mess may be in reference to its appearance or an archaic word for a quantity of food.

Sussex pond pudding – A suet-pastry-encased lemon with butter and sugar, boiled or steamed for several hours. The 'pond' is the thick sauce created whilst the pudding is cooked, which oozes out when it is cut. Unsurprisingly originating from the county of Sussex, its earliest incarnations (such as from Hannah Woolley's *The Queen-like Closet*, 1672) did not include the lemon.

There is only one antidote for a day like that: chocolate. I needed comfort food and I needed it fast.

Elizabeth Bard, *Lunch in Paris*

Liquid delectable, I love thy brown
  Deep-glimmering color like a wood-nymph's tress;
  Potent and swift to urge on Love's excess,
Thou wert most loved in the fair Aztec town...

Francis Saltus Saltus, from 'Ode To Chocolate'

SWEET NOSTALGIA – LOST PLEASURES...

Spangles – Made by Mars from 1950 to the early 1980s, these fruit-flavoured boiled sweets, individually wrapped and sold in a tube, were released in many varieties, including Old English Spangles, with such flavours as butterscotch and pear drops, and Mystery Spangles, the flavour of which was never revealed.

Fry's Five Centres – A variation of Fry's Chocolate Cream, one of the first chocolate bars created by the pioneer of mass-produced chocolate bars, J. S. Fry & Sons. For this variation the fondant centre of each section had a different flavour: raspberry, lime, vanilla, coffee and orange. It launched in 1934 and was discontinued in 1992.

Cadbury Fuse – The Fuse bar was made of solid chocolate, and contained raisins, fudge, nuts and crisp cereal suspended within it. It was introduced in 1996 with a huge marketing campaign and to great success, but discontinued ten years later.

Pacers – Originally launched as Opal Mints, these minty sweets were the same shape and texture as Opal Fruits (now Starburst). When they were rebranded as Pacers, they were white with a green stripe through them.

SYNSEPALUM DULCIFICUM

It doesn't sound easy on the tongue, but it actually is! Also known as the miracle berry, this West African fruit contains a substance called miraculin which, when eaten, binds itself to the taste buds and distorts the taste of sour foods, making lemons taste like toffee. In the 1970s, the concept of the 'miraculin party' was popular, in which people would get together, eat some of the fruit in pill form, and try various foods. Where it grows locally, it is used to sweeten products such as palm wine, and in Japan it is commonly used by dieters and diabetics.

WHAT'S IN A NAME?

Maid of honour tarts – Various stories associate these tarts with Anne Boleyn, the second wife of Henry VIII and maid of honour to his first wife, Catherine of Aragon. They are also known as Richmond Tarts, after Richmond on the outskirts of London, where Henry VIII built a palace and where there is a road named Maids of Honour Row, built for the ladies-in-waiting of George II's wife. The tarts are made of shortcrust or puff pastry and are filled with almond custard.

Fruit fool – A dish consisting of puréed fruits, whipped cream and sugar. The earliest record of a dish called a fool is from 1598. The name may come from the French *fouler* meaning to press or mash, or have a similar basis as trifle, implying it has little substance.

Tarte tatin – Accidentally invented by French hotelier Stephine Tatin (1838–1917), this upside-down tart is said to have been created in 1898 as an attempt to salvage a dessert gone awry.

Peach Melba – In 1892/3, chef *Auguste Escoffier* of the Savoy Hotel was so enchanted when he heard *Dame Nellie Melba* singing at Covent Garden that he named a dessert after her. In its original form, the dish included a swan sculpted from ice to resemble the one in the opera in which Escoffier had seen Melba perform.

*Her cooking was always delicious,
partly I think from the fresh
country ingredients, and as I read
her letters I could almost taste
the Jersey cream and rich
brown sugar in my mouth.*

DIANA DUFF, *LEAVES FROM THE FIG TREE*

PLEASE WITH CHEESE

Cheese is milk's leap towards immortality.

CLIFTON FADIMAN

SAY CHEESE! SOME FAVOURITES

Cheddar – The UK's favourite, a reasonably hard cheese originating in the Somerset village of Cheddar, it has been in production since at least the twelfth century, though the recipe may have arrived with the Romans. In 1170, Henry II purchased 10,420 pounds of Cheddar. The caves of Cheddar Gorge provided the ideal humidity and temperature for it to mature. Captain Robert Falcon Scott took 3,500 pounds of the cheese on his ill-fated Antarctic expedition in 1901.

Halloumi – A Cypriot cheese made from a combination of sheep and goat's milk. It is stored in brine, giving it a rather salty taste. It has a high melting point, making it ideal for frying or grilling.

Paneer – An Indian cheese, made by curdling milk with lemon juice. Like halloumi, it has a high melting point and can be cooked with ease, including in curry dishes.

Mozzarella – Traditionally produced from the milk of water buffalo, mozzarella is a semi-soft cheese originating from Italy. Its name comes from a Neapolitan word meaning 'cut', as the process of creating the cheese involves it being cut into smaller pieces.

Mascarpone – Also from Italy, mascarpone's high butterfat content classifies it as a triple-cream cheese. It is made from crème fraiche, and is often used in sweet as well as savoury dishes.

Edam – A Dutch cheese that is sold in spheres encased in coloured paraffin wax, it has a low fat content and is therefore softer than other 'hard' cheeses. It ages and travels well, which made it incredibly popular between the fourteenth and eighteenth centuries, especially on long sea voyages.

*How can anyone govern a nation
that has two hundred and
forty-six different kinds
of cheese?*

CHARLES DE GAULLE

We have seen thee, queen of cheese,
Lying quietly at your ease,
Gently fanned by evening breeze,
Thy fair form no flies dare seize.

All gaily dressed soon you'll go
To the great Provincial show,
To be admired by many a beau
In the city of Toronto.

Cows numerous as a swarm of bees,
Or as the leaves upon the trees,
It did require to make thee please,
And stand unrivalled, queen of cheese.

JAMES MCINTYRE, FROM 'ODE ON THE MAMMOTH
CHEESE WEIGHING OVER 7,000 POUNDS'

As for butter versus margarine,
trust cows more than chemists.

JOAN DYE GUSSOW

Blue cheese contains natural amphetamines.
Why are students not informed about this?

MARK E. SMITH

SAY IT WITH CHEESE – PRESENTATION

Good food is only half the battle at a dinner party – if you want to stand out as the *big cheese* then presentation must be picture-perfect. If your guests think you haven't put in the effort or you're *cheese-paring* then they could get *cheesed off*. The food may taste great but if it looks like it has been thrown together then it just won't *cut the cheese* and for you that's *tough cheese*. Before you eat take a photo of your guests with their delightful plates and remind them to say *cheese*.

RAW MILK

Raw milk is milk that has been neither pasteurised nor homogenised. Pasteurisation is a process that involves heating milk for a very short amount of time then rapidly cooling it in order to kill off harmful bacteria that may be present. Homogenisation is a process in which the fat globules that sit on the top of unprocessed milk as a layer of cream are broken up so they stay suspended throughout the milk. This is done by pressurising heated milk and forcing it through small holes, and is used to extend milk's shelf life and remove the need to stir in the layer of cream when the milk is to be used. The sale of raw milk is restricted or banned in some countries, and in England it may only be bought directly from farmers who must adhere to a very high level of hygiene. However, in France, the production of cheese from anything but raw milk is considered sacrilegious, and in Germany raw milk and its cheese are promoted strongly by the health food movement.

CHEESE ROLLING

Chasing a wheel of cheese down a hill. Is there any more noble pursuit? Of course not. That's why two separate British villages do it annually. Both Cooper's Hill, Gloucestershire, and Stilton, Cambridgeshire, hold competitions in which cheese is chased down a hill, for fun and the pursuit of cheese. Cheese rolling has also become popular in Japan, though there they prefer to use artificial cheese (thus, some would say, missing the point slightly).

For lunch, he said, we could have biscuits,
cold meat, bread and butter, and jam – but
no cheese. Cheese, like oil, makes too much of
itself. It wants the whole boat to itself. It goes
through the hamper, and gives a cheesy flavour
to everything else there. You can't tell whether
you are eating apple pie, or German sausage,
or strawberries and cream. It all seems cheese.
There's too much odour about cheese.

JEROME K. JEROME, *THREE MEN IN A BOAT*

DORSET BLUE VINNEY

The word vinney comes from either the obsolete Dorset term 'vinew', meaning to become mouldy, or a corruption of the word veiny, referencing the blue veins in the cheese. The cheese has been common in Dorset for hundreds of years, and was mentioned by the nineteenth-century poet, William Barnes.

What's the only cheese that can hide a horse?
Mascarpone.

COOKS' TIPS – CHEESE COURSE ETIQUETTE

- ◉ The amount of cheese on a cheeseboard is not the amount that is intended to be eaten; it is left as whole as possible to keep the integrity of the cheese.

- ◉ A variety of knives and tools are available, depending on the type of cheese; the roquefortaise is a wire guillotine for cutting softer cheese, such as Roquefort, whereas some of the harder cheeses may require a two-handled knife.

- ◉ If you don't have specialised knives for each cheese, don't mix knives; try to use one knife for softer cheese and one for the harder cheeses.

- ◉ It is completely up to you whether you choose to eat the rind of any cheese. As cheese mostly matures from the outside in, the rind will have a more developed and mature taste, but may be brittle, dry or bitter.

- ◉ Cheese with a rind should be cut in a way that ensures all tasters have a section with rind, as regardless of whether they will eat the rind itself, the flavour of the cheese changes as it gets closer to the rind. Therefore, if the cheese is wedge-shaped, don't cut the tip off but take a slice from the side.

Stilton, thou shouldst be living at this hour
And so thou art. Nor losest grace thereby;
England has need of thee, and so have I—
She is a Fen. Far as the eye can scour,
League after grassy league from Lincoln tower
To Stilton in the fields, she is a Fen.
Yet this high cheese, by choice of fenland men,
Like a tall green volcano rose in power.
Plain living and long drinking are no more,
And pure religion reading "Household Words",
And sturdy manhood sitting still all day
Shrink, like this cheese that crumbles to its core;
While my digestion, like the House of Lords,
The heaviest burdens on herself doth lay.

G. K. CHESTERTON, FROM 'SONNET TO A STILTON CHEESE'

Controversial Foods

What is food to one,
is to others bitter poison.

Lucretius

BANNED FOODS

Sausages – Roman Emperor Constantine I banned sausages and decreed it a sin to eat one because of their link to pagan festivals. Sausage eating remained a secretive and dangerous pleasure.

Eccles cakes – Declared off limits by Oliver Cromwell (1599–1658) during his tenure as Lord Protector of England, Scotland and Ireland, Eccles cakes were considered too rich and sumptuous and to have pagan significance.

Christmas dinner – Seeking to bring the focus of Christmas back to the birth of Jesus, Oliver Cromwell also ordered soldiers to confiscate food being prepared to celebrate the event.

Chewing gum – Due to problems with improper disposal and vandalism, chewing gum was outlawed in Singapore in 1992. However, since 2004, the government has allowed gum with medicinal and dental uses to be chewed.

Haggis – The import of the Scottish offal dish to America was prohibited in 1971. Sadly, the traditional Burns' night fare is still unavailable within the United States.

Pufferfish

Fugu – A number of restaurants in the US as well as Japan are licensed to serve Japanese puffer fish (fugu), but it is banned in the EU. Fugu contains lethal amounts of tetrodotoxin in its liver, skin and ovaries, a poison which – if the delicacy is prepared incorrectly – can lead to paralysis, asphyxiation and eventually death.

Ortolans – These small birds are kept in artificial light and force fed with millet until they become outrageously fat, then drowned in Almanac, plucked and roasted, to be eaten whole, beak, bones and all. The trick is to suck the hot yellow fat from the body and then slowly crunch the remains. This dish has now been banned in France to protect the species but it is still legal in the UK.

Absinthe – In its original form, this spirit was the muse for many great geniuses such as Vincent Van Gogh and Oscar Wilde. It contained the chemical compound thujone, associated with mental illness, intense creativity and hallucinations. In the early twentieth century many countries outlawed it. Though it is now legalised almost worldwide, thujone levels are regulated and it is not made to the same recipe.

Who can believe with common sense,
A bacon slice gives God offence;
Or, how a herring has a charm
Almighty vengeance to disarm?
Wrapp'd up in Majesty divine,
Does he regard on what we dine?

JONATHAN SWIFT, 'EPIGRAM FROM THE FRENCH'

VICTORIAN METHODS OF DETECTING ADULTERATED FOOD

To detect adulterated wine – *Heat equal parts of oyster-shells and sulphur together, and keep them in a white heat for fifteen minutes, and when cold, mix them with an equal quantity of cream of tartar; put this mixture into a strong bottle with common water to boil for one hour, and then decant into ounce phials, and add 20 drops of muriatic acid to each; this liquor precipitates the least quantity of lead, copper, &c. from wines in a very sensible black precipitate.*

To test the purity of flour – *Grasp a handful briskly, and squeeze it half a minute: if genuine, it will preserve the form of the cavity of the hand, even though rudely placed on a table; if adulterated, it will almost immediately fall down.*

SAMUEL AND SARAH ADAMS, *THE COMPLETE SERVANT*

BIZARRE FOODS

Would you try… sannakji?
What: Small live octopuses
Where: South Korea
How: The little octopuses, about the size of the palm of your hand, are taken live from a tank of water, chopped up and taken to the table, tentacles still squirming. With chopsticks you skilfully pick up the little pieces of wiggling tentacles and place in your mouth. Be very careful to chew thoroughly though, as if swallowed straight away the suckers can stick to your throat and choke you to death. More than a few people have finished their last meal this way.

Would you try… cuy?
What: Guinea pig
Where: Peru
How: These rodents look very cute and make lovely pets but in some places they also make a tasty meal. Because they are small, easy to look after and breed very quickly, guinea pigs are economical to keep and are used for trading by many households in Peru and Bolivia. However, when you order one, be prepared – it is not just a fillet steak that is served up but the entire animal, which looks like it has been flattened with a rolling pin; head, teeth and all.

Would you try... frog sashimi?
What: Beating frog heart
Where: Japan
How: An almost live dish. The frog is killed in front of you and the heart taken out and handed to you on a plate. This delicacy is so fresh that the little red heart is still visibly beating up and down. Next, using your chopsticks, delicately pick it up (you don't want to stop it beating) put it in your mouth and eat it. It's so small it'll be gone in a heartbeat. This delightful appetiser can be followed up with the rest of the frog carcass served raw on a bed of its own skin.

Would you try... Casu Marzu?
What: Cheese filled with maggots
Where: Sardinia, Italy
How: Pecorino is a traditional Sardinian cheese made from sheep's milk which can be turned into Casu Marzu. The pecorino is left outside to attract the attention of cheese flies which lay thousands of eggs, which turn into insect larvae that digest and break down the fat of the cheese. When the block of cheese is full of maggots it is ready to eat but make sure the maggots are not dead as then the food is considered unsafe. Casu Marzu can be eaten with or without the maggots depending on your preference. Be careful when eating with maggots, though; they can jump up to 6 inches when disturbed.

Would you try... Very Peculiar?

What: A chocolate bar made with Marmite

Where: UK

How: Sweet milk chocolate combined with the savoury yeast-powered might of Marmite; let's face it, you're either going to love it or hate it. Even those who love the stuff might wonder at this concoction. The preparation is easy; buy it, break a bit off and put it in your mouth, then either do the same thing again or run to the bathroom and wash your mouth out with soap.

Would you try... durian?

What: A thorn-covered fruit with a very strong odour

Where: South East Asia

How: If you're walking through a street market in Indonesia or Malaysia and it suddenly smells like a sewage plant has exploded, it's possible someone nearby is selling durian. The flavour is often described as delicious but the odour has been compared to (hold your breath) rotten onions, pig excrement, skunk spray, dead fish, very old socks and rotting flesh covered in vomit. The fruit has been banned in some public places for obvious reasons so if you do buy it be careful where you take it.

Would you try... balut?

What: A fertilised duck or chicken egg

Where: The Philippines

How: An egg that is unlike other eggs because it has been fertilised and the baby duck or chicken has been growing inside. When the egg is seventeen days old it is considered the prime time for cooking, before all the chick's features become fully developed. It is boiled in the same way as a normal egg and placed in sand to keep it warm, eaten with the shell on, and best accompanied by salt, chilli and vinegar.

Would you try... salo?

What: A slab of fat

Where: Ukraine

How: That's pretty much it. Salo is just a lump of fat from a pig and can be eaten raw, smoked or cooked. It is often covered with salt, pepper, garlic and paprika to make it extra tasty and can be stored for up to a year.

What's yellow and dangerous?
Shark infested custard.

THE ORIGINS OF FANTA

With the outbreak of World War Two, The Coca-Cola Company's operations in Germany were completely cut off from their headquarters in Atlanta, Georgia. Max Keith, head of Coca-Cola in Germany, aimed to stay loyal to the company, and as much as possible to keep the business going. Unfortunately, the ingredients needed to manufacture Coke were in short supply, so Keith invented a new soft drink, using only ingredients that were available in Nazi Germany, mostly leftovers from other food industries. In naming this new drink, he instructed his staff to let their fantasies, or *fantasie*, run wild: hence the name, Fanta. When the war was over, Keith's operation was reintegrated with the rest of The Coca-Cola Company, and Fanta was added to the roster of Coca-Cola drinks.

GM FOODS

GM foods are foods that have been genetically modified, through scientists inserting or deleting genes from their DNA. Traits that have been given to foods include resistance to pesticides and viruses and higher nutritional content. GM corporations assert that genetically modified foods have been proven safe; however, consumer rights groups and environmentalist groups such as Greenpeace accuse them of blocking any sort of independent research into their effects, and claim that GM foods may have unexpected effects on the ecosystems into which they are introduced.

FICTIONAL GOURMANDS

Hannibal Lecter – Created by author Thomas Harris and portrayed famously by Anthony Hopkins, Hannibal Lecter is a sophisticated serial killer who enjoys fine wine, fine music and fine food, which includes the flesh of his victims.

Jabba the Hutt – A crime lord from George Lucas's *Star Wars* trilogy, known for greed and gluttony; he is even known to eat his enemies and cohorts.

Patrick Bateman – From Bret Easton Ellis's controversial 1991 book *American Psycho*, Bateman is a late 1980s banker on Wall Street. Epitomising the yuppie culture prevalent at the time, Bateman is obsessed with eating at the finest of New York's restaurants, and using only the finest ingredients in his own cooking. His only passions that come close to competing are his interest in high fashion and committing incredibly gruesome murders.

John Self – The main character in Martin Amis's 1984 novel *Money*, John Self is a director of TV adverts who is moving into directing feature films. His main joys in life include smoking, drinking, money, sex and fast food, including the Long Whopper and the Rumpburger.

What's in
Your Kitchen?

*If you can't stand the heat,
get out of the kitchen.*

Harry S. Truman

THE GOOD KNIFE GUIDE

One of the staple items to be found in most kitchens is the great big knife block with knives of every shape, size, religion and creed bursting out of it, but have you ever harboured the thought that you may not need all of them? Here's a handy guide to which knives you actually need and which ones you can sell to the local unambitious sword swallower:

Chef's knife – This is the most important knife in the kitchen. It can be used to mince, dice, slice and chop, which is why it's worth spending some time finding a good one.

Paring knife – This small knife can be used for the more fiddly jobs such as chopping garlic or trimming the fat off meat. They are usually about 3–5 inches long, with a straight edge and a very sharp blade.

Serrated knife – This knife has saw-like teeth. It is used for slicing bread and other large items, but don't worry about spending a lot on one. Serrated knives are difficult to sharpen and therefore need replacing fairly regularly, making a cheaper choice the most sensible.

ALTERNATIVE HOME-COOKING...

Fish in the dish... washer – Wrap your fish fillet securely in tinfoil along with some lemon and butter, place it in the top rack of your dishwasher and set it on the hottest cycle. At the end of the cycle you should have a perfectly done piece of fish. DO NOT ADD ANY SOAP OR DETERGENT.

Iron chef – Cooking anything on an upside-down iron would be a little tricky but using an iron to toast a sandwich is surprisingly efficient and easy. Take your regular cheese sandwich and pop it in a paper bag, place it on top of a folded newspaper and then grab your iron. Set your iron to a low temperature and place it onto your sandwich for a couple of minutes, turn the sandwich over and repeat.

COOKS' TIPS – SAVING ON ELBOW GREASE

⊙ One proven way to tackle a dirty oven is to add one tablespoon of caustic soda to hot water. However, be sure to do it this way around and not add the water to the soda as this will create an eruption of hot caustic solution capable of causing very serious burns.

⊙ To clean up a blackened aluminium pan, boil the leaves and trimmings of some rhubarb and then leave them to sit in the pan. Give the pan a thorough rinse after doing this because the leaves are poisonous.

⊙ To remove marks from the inside of a mug try using toothpaste. Any marks made by metal cutlery will soon vanish and your mug will be left with that squeaky clean minty sheen.

⊙ To clean out a teapot, pour equal parts boiling water and vinegar into it and leave to stand for 10 minutes.

⊙ Rubbing your cutlery with a cork from a wine bottle will restore them to their shiny best.

⊙ Get an old soapy cloth and pop it in your microwave. Turn your microwave on full power for two or three minutes and then leave the door closed for about five minutes afterwards. This will steam clean your microwave and allow you to easily wipe the dirt off.

Kitchen Fads and Fancies

Spurtle – A Scottish invention, this utensil resembles a wooden dowel and is used for stirring soups and porridges. A Golden Spurtle is awarded to the winner of the annual World Porridge Making Championships.

Chocolate fountain – Invented in the 1920s by Ben Brisman, it didn't become popular until the second half of the century. It creates a continuous waterfall of liquid chocolate to dip marshmallows or fruit in. The high viscosity of most melted chocolate is a problem, requiring the addition of vegetable oil or the use of more expensive couverture chocolate.

Glass rolling pin – A hollow glass rolling pin, made as such to allow it to be filled with cold water or ice to assist in keeping pastry dough cold while it is being manipulated.

Oyster shucker – Somewhere between a knife and spoon, an oyster shucker usually consists of a wooden handle with a rounded blade used for opening and removing the meat from oysters.

Honey dipper – A sphere with grooves in on a stick: when the dipper is held so the grooves are horizontal, the honey will not drip from the implement, making it a cleaner method than using a spoon.

Cherry stoner – Also known as a cherry pitter, this removes the stone from the cherry whilst leaving the cherry relatively intact.

SOMETHING FISHY

In the hands of an able cook, fish can become an inexhaustible source of perpetual delight.

JEAN-ANTHELME BRILLAT-SAVARIN

SUSHI FACTS

The history of sushi actually began in China, not Japan as one would expect. It was originally a second-century way of preserving fish. Though most people associate sushi with raw fish, it is actually the sticky rice dressed with vinegar that is the integral and defining factor in whether a dish is sushi.

Sushi in Japan can be traced back to the seventh century, when a reference to it was included in a document about tax.

Modern sushi was invented by Hanaya Yohei (1799–1858), who removed the fermentation and preservation element from the dish.

Sushi chefs, until recently, had to train for ten years before beginning work. Due to the recent explosion in popularity of sushi, in practice this is now cut short to two years.

Dance to your daddy,
My little laddy,
Dance to your daddy, my little lamb;
You shall have a fishy
In a little dishy,
You shall have a fishy when the boat comes in.

TRADITIONAL ENGLISH FOLK SONG

SAY IT WITH FISH –
A ROMANTIC DINNER FOR TWO

When a romantic meal goes well it feels *like shooting a fish in a barrel* but when it goes wrong you can feel like a *fish out of water*. You may think you're *a big fish in a small pond* while romantically wooing across the table but if the food and the mood are not right it can be a whole *different kettle of fish*. You will soon feel like a *fish in troubled waters* and the one you want may feel like they have *bigger fish to fry*. So prepare in detail then relax with a drink (though not *like a fish*). Remark to your guest that they look great and you hope they enjoyed the meal, but don't *fish for compliments*. Hopefully your hook and bait will be enough to reel them in but if it's a *cold fish* don't worry; *there are plenty more fish in the sea*.

*Fish, to taste right, must swim three times –
in water, in butter and in wine.*

POLISH PROVERB

We also learned that Spigola con Finocchio
Selvatico, *sea bass with wild fennel, was the
main course on the menu. It made her salivate
enviously, she said. Sea bass was an expensive
luxury she couldn't afford.*

VIDA ADAMOLI, *LA BELLA VITA*

What's in a Name?

Arbroath smokie – A speciality of Arbroath in Angus, Scotland. The legend goes that a building containing haddock being preserved in salt set fire one night, and on inspection the haddock in the burnt barrels tasted delicious. This process was adjusted to avoid the destruction of property and has been in use ever since.

Bismarck herring – Marinated herring in vinegar, sold by Johann Wiechmann in Stralsund, Germany. Wiechmann admired the chancellor of the German Empire, Otto von Bismarck, and sent him a barrel of the herrings for his enjoyment and a letter asking if the herring could be named after him. The chancellor agreed and the herring still have that name to this day.

What's the worst thing about being an octopus?
Washing your hands before dinner.

I will not eat oysters. I want my food dead –
not sick, not wounded – dead.

WOODY ALLEN

JELLIED EELS

A traditional East End dish from the eighteenth century that was previously widely eaten but has since waned in popularity, jellied eels are still available in a few Eel Pie & Mash Houses in London, the oldest shop surviving since 1891. They are simply made by chopping up the eels into approximate round shapes and boiling them. Vinegar, stock and spices are added to the water and that combined with the natural gelatin of the fish forms a jelly when the mix cools.

EEL BROTH

Ingredients: ½ lb. of eels, a small bunch of sweet herbs, including parsley; ½ onion, 10 peppercorns, 3 pints of water, 2 cloves, salt and pepper to taste.

Mode: After having cleaned and skinned the eel, cut it into small pieces, and put it into a stewpan with the other ingredients; simmer gently until the liquid is reduced nearly half, carefully removing the scum as it rises. Strain it through a hair-sieve; put it by in a cool place, and, when wanted, take off all the fat from the top, warm up as much as is required, and serve with sippets of toasted bread. This is a very nutritious broth, and easy of digestion.

Time: To be simmered until the liquor is reduced to half.
Average cost: 6d.
Sufficient: to make 1 ½ pint of broth.
Seasonable from June to March.

ISABELLA BEETON, *THE BOOK OF HOUSEHOLD MANAGEMENT*

From the Sublime to the Ridiculous

*Part of the secret of success in life
is to eat what you like and let
the food fight it out inside.*

Mark Twain

MISNOMERS

Bombay duck – This animal may be from Bombay, but it is most certainly not a duck. It is actually a lizardfish (which, to clarify, is a type of fish rather than a type of lizard).

Buffalo wings – These chicken wings are fried then coated in a hot cayenne pepper sauce, and were in fact never attached to a buffalo. They were invented in the city of Buffalo, New York.

Mock turtle soup – This soup was created in the eighteenth century as an imitation of the much more expensive turtle soup. The offal of a calf and oysters replace the turtle meat. The Mock Turtle in Lewis Carroll's *Alice's Adventures in Wonderland* has the head and feet of a calf and the body of a turtle, supposedly being the animal mock turtle soup is made from.

Halve Hahn – A German phrase literally translated as 'half a rooster'; however, if you were to order it in Cologne, you would get something slightly less filling. Based on variations of the phrase *'Kann isch ne halve han?'* which means 'Can I get a half (of a sandwich)?', it has come to refer to half a cheese roll.

Rocky Mountain oysters – Also known as prairie oysters or cowboy caviar, these are bull testicles, usually deep-fried and served with a cocktail sauce dip but sometimes served in a demi-glace.

BIGGEST FOODS EVER

Largest omelette – The biggest omelette ever was made in Turkey for World Egg Day 2010. It measured 10 metres in diameter, included 110,010 eggs and took two and a half hours to cook.

Largest slab of fudge – Weighing in at 2.35 tonnes, the largest slab of fudge ever was cooked up by William Nicklosovich and Peppermint Jim Cosby in 2009, in Michigan, USA.

Largest cheese – The largest slice of cheese ever churned was unveiled in 2007 by a New York cheese shop and a Danish cheesemaker. It weighed 1,323 pounds and measured 6 feet wide.

Largest sandwich – The largest sandwich ever was made in Mexico City in 2004, and weighed 6,991 pounds.

Largest chocolate bar – Created in Armenia in 2010 with cocoa beans imported from Ghana, this chocolate bar weighed 9,702 pounds and measured 5.6 metres long.

Largest bagel – Baked for the New York State Fair in 2004, this colossal bagel weighed 868 pounds and was 6 feet in diameter.

THAT'S NOT FOOD!
(OR THE FRENCH WILL EAT ANYTHING)

Monsieur Mangetout (1950–2007)

Born Michel Lotito, this man was known for his incredible ability to eat anything. This began in his childhood in France, and his crowning achievement was his deconstruction and ingestion of a whole two-seater airplane over the course of two years. Despite his ability to eat normally poisonous material with no ill effects, both bananas and hard-boiled eggs were known to make him sick. Doctors found he had unusually powerful digestive juices and stomach and intestine lining twice as thick as normal.

Tarrare (c. 1772–1798)

The late-eighteenth-century French showman and soldier had a gruesome and insatiable appetite. Kicked out of the family home as a teenager due to his parents' inability to afford to feed him, he began associating with thieves and others on the fringes of society. His ability to swallow live animals and various non-foods such as corks and stones led him to become a street performer in Paris. He later joined the French Revolutionary Army, but the rations could not sate his hunger and he was hospitalised suffering from exhaustion. Doctors tested his eating capacity, showing him capable of eating a live cat, a meal for fifteen labourers, lizards, puppies and eels. Once he was even accused of eating a toddler. He eventually died of tuberculosis. No explanation was ever found for his condition.

Charles Domery (c. 1778–1800)

Also a member of the French Revolutionary Army in the late eighteenth century, Domery was born in Poland but deserted the Prussian Army in order to seek out larger rations. He was recorded to eat on average fourteen cats a month over a year while stationed near Paris, and was known to eat grass if other food was not available. When on board a frigate, he attempted to eat the leg of a crewmate, which had been severed by a cannonball. After being captured by the British, in a test of his eating capacity he consumed a total of 16 pounds of raw meat and tallow candles and four bottles of porter in one day.

BIZARRE FOOD EVENTS

Egg throwing – A mixture of various egg-based sports make up the World Egg Throwing Championship, held annually in Swaton, Lincolnshire. These include egg and spoon relays, machine-assisted egg hurling and egg catching, an event liable to leave the less skilled participants with egg on their face.

La Tomatina – Every year on the last Wednesday of August, the Spanish town of Buñol, Valencia, holds what can only be described as a council-sponsored food fight. Truckloads of tomatoes, grown specifically for the event, are dumped in the town square, which marks the beginning of an hour-long tomato fight.

Pancake race – These events are quite typical for Shrove Tuesday (Pancake Day); however, the festivities held in Olney, Buckinghamshire, have a slight twist. Since 1445, the townswomen have raced through the town, frying pan in hand, to the parish church. In 1950, the town of Liberal, USA, challenged Olney to see who was fastest over the same distance with a frying pan, and now the overall winner is the fastest of both races.

Bun fight – Whenever a significant event for celebration happens in Abingdon, Oxfordshire, such as a royal wedding, the millennium, or the town being granted a Royal Charter, the town council and mayor celebrate by throwing buns off the County Hall Museum. This has been done since the coronation of George III in 1761.

Battle of the Oranges – Ivrea, near Turin, holds a yearly carnival that includes a massive orange fight. The fight is held to commemorate the overthrowing of two tyrants in the twelfth and thirteenth centuries, the first of whom was said to have been decapitated by a young commoner he tried to rape. The two teams represent the tyrants' guards and the rebels.

A Fitless Cock by Any Other Name

Fitless Cock – oatmeal and onion pudding

Clapshot – mashed potato and swede

The Dean's Cream – a trifle-like pudding

Wet Nelly – northern English bread-based pudding

Aberdeen Nips – smoked haddock on toast

Girdle Sponge – fried sponge cake

Flummery – stewed fruit pudding

Inky-Pinky – leftover beef hash

Huffkin – Kentish bread roll made with milk

Wow-wow Sauce – port and wine vinegar sauce

Scotch Woodcock – toast with scrambled egg and anchovy paste

Love in Disguise – stuffed cow heart

FOOD STATISTICS

- ◉ Nearly four in ten British people do not cook their evening meal during the week, instead choosing quick, ready-made options and leftovers.

- ◉ Every year, 8.3 million tonnes of food and drink is wasted in UK homes.

- ◉ The most expensive food ever sold is the Italian white Alba truffle, which has been bought for over £80,000 per kilogram.

- ◉ Sugar cane is the world's most prevalent crop, with 1,324 million metric tons produced annually.

- ◉ The Czech Republic annually drinks an average of 276.1 pints of beer per person, the highest amount in the world.

- ◉ The most common food allergy is to cow's milk. This is much more common in Asia and Africa than Europe.

- ◉ Switzerland eats the most chocolate per head of any country, averaging 11.4 kilograms per year.

- ◉ The heaviest potato on record was grown in Lebanon and weighed 11.3 kilograms.

- ◉ Hot dogs are the cause of 17 per cent of deaths from choking.

Fad Diets

Times have changed greatly since William the Conqueror, he of the Norman Conquest, attempted to lose weight by consuming nothing but alcohol. Here are some other interesting dietary ideas that have (or have not) caught on over the years:

- Both Kellogg's Corn Flakes and the American graham cracker were originally intended to help dampen the libido.

- The poet Lord Byron popularised a vinegar diet, which involved the ingestion of copious amounts of vinegar in order to lose weight and maintain a pale complexion.

- Created by Seth Roberts, a psychology professor at Tsinghua University, the Shangri-La Diet suggests consuming between 100 and 400 of one's daily calories through flavourless foods such as extra light olive oil or fructose and water. This, Roberts proposes, will suppress the appetite and lower the 'set point' that the body perceives as its ideal weight.

- Some Australians are known to practise Kangatarianism: the only meat they will consume is that from a kangaroo, as they view it as having a low environmental and ecological impact as well as being more humane than other meats.

- Horace Fletcher (1849–1919) recommended at least thirty-two chews per mouthful, including solids and liquids.

Baby and I
Were baked in a pie,
The gravy was wonderful hot.
We had nothing to pay
To the baker that day
And so we crept out of the pot.

TRADITIONAL NURSERY RHYME

Preserving and Storing Food

Marmalade in the morning has the same effect on taste buds that a cold shower has on the body.

Jeanine Larmoth

COOKS' TIPS – KEEPING IT CHILLED

⊙ Never leave an open tin in the fridge – it can corrode and spoil the food.

⊙ Wrap food before placing it in the fridge. This will keep smells to a minimum and protect the food from the dry air in the fridge.

⊙ Food that should not be put in the fridge: tomatoes (they go woolly), potatoes (they sprout), bread (it goes stale quicker in the fridge than in a bread bin), bananas (they go black) and mushrooms (they are best stored in a cool, dry place, e.g. a cupboard).

⊙ Don't put hot food in the fridge; it will cause condensation and raise the temperature of the fridge, possibly compromising the other food.

⊙ Do not overcrowd the fridge, as this will reduce air circulation and cooling.

⊙ Eradicate odours by placing a piece of charcoal in your fridge.

SAY IT WITH PIES – STORING YOUR FOOD

The thought of storing food correctly and safely turns many of us *pie-eyed* but if you don't do it you could have your *finger in a lot of pies* before you find what you want. Some people just chuck their shopping anywhere and end up eating *humble pie* when they can't find what they are looking for and what they can find is well out of date. Having a tried and tested system is not *pie in the sky* but *easy as pie* when you use labels. Simply write the content and date on the package and when you cook the food it will be as *nice as pie.*

For a ham twenty-four pounds in weight, take two ounces of saltpetre, half a pound of common salt, one pound of bay salt, and one ounce of black pepper. Mix these together, and rub them well into the ham: then let it stand three days, and at the expiration of that time pour one pound of treacle over it, and let it remain twenty-four hours; after that time, let it be turned every day for a month, and each time rub the liquor well into it. After this, steep the ham in cold water for twelve hours, then dry it well and hang it up. It will not require any further steeping when it is to be boiled; and it should be boiled slowly, say at the rate of about three hours for a ham of the weight of ten pounds.

JANE LOUDON, *THE LADY'S COUNTRY COMPANION*

COOKS' TIPS – THE BIG FREEZE

⊙ If something needs to be frozen quickly, then do not place large amounts of unfrozen food in the freezer at once as this will raise its temperature, slowing the freezing process.

⊙ Label the things in your freezer, as when frozen it is not easy to work out what an item is.

⊙ If food is not appropriately wrapped then the air that circulates round the freezer will give it 'freezer burn'.

⊙ Keep your freezer full; they run more efficiently when they are well-filled.

⊙ Liquids expand when frozen. Leave a space in anything containing liquid to allow for this.

⊙ Foods that should not be put in the freezer: whole eggs (they will burst), previously frozen food that has not yet been cooked, various raw fruit and vegetables (including tomatoes, cabbages, onions and melons), certain dairy products (such as custard, yoghurt and single and soured cream – double cream and pasteurised milk can be frozen), mayonnaise and cake mixture.

⊙ Keep a stock book so you know what you have in your freezer and where everything has been stored.

Bread requires almost as much care as milk to preserve it wholesome and fresh. It should be laid, as soon as it is perfectly cold, into a large earthen pan with a cover, which should be kept free from crumbs, and be frequently scalded, and then wiped very dry for use. Loaves which have been cut should have a smaller pan appropriated to them, and this also should have the loose crumbs wiped from it daily. It is a good plan to raise the bread-pans from the floor of the larder, when there is no proper stand or frame for the purpose, by means of two flat wedges of wood, so as to allow a current of air to pass under them.

ELIZA ACTON, *MODERN COOKERY FOR PRIVATE FAMILIES*

Maximum Recommended Fridge Storage Times

Product	Days (approx.)
Milk	4–5
Cheese, soft	2–3
Cheese, hard	7–14
Fruit juice, freshly squeezed	1–2
Eggs, raw	14
Vegetables, cooked	2
Potatoes, cooked	2
Joints (e.g. lamb, beef), cooked	3
Joints (e.g. lamb, beef), raw	3
Ham, cooked	2
Casserole, cooked	2
Sliced meat, cooked	2
Fish, cooked	1
Fish, raw	1–2
Poultry, raw	2
Sliced meat, raw	2
Mince, raw	1
Sausages, raw	3
Bacon, raw	7

Apply with a brush a solution of gum-arabic to the shells, or immerse the eggs therein, let them dry, and afterwards park them in dry charcoal dust. This prevents their being affected by any alterations of temperature.

JAMES W. LAUGHTON ON THE PRESERVATION OF EGGS,
THE GENERAL RECEIPT BOOK

MAXIMUM RECOMMENDED FREEZER STORAGE TIMES

Product	Months (approx.)
Milk	6–7
Cheese, hard	4–5
Cheese, soft	3–4
Ice cream	3–5
Beef	4–6
Chicken	10–12
Lamb	4–5
Pork	4–6
Venison	10–11
Minced beef	3–4
Green vegetables	10–12
Tomatoes	6–7
Fruit juice	4–5
Bread	2–3
Ready-prepared meals	2–5
Oily fish	3–4
White fish	6–7

(Times are for an average domestic freezer.)

THE GREAT OUTDOORS

*Give me books, French wine, fruit, fine weather
and a little music played out of doors by
somebody I do not know.*

JOHN KEATS

FORAGING

Why buy food when you can find it? Foraging gives you food that is free of preservatives, free of packaging and – well, free! Here are some wild foods that can be found in the British countryside and seaside – though take care to identify seafood, mushrooms and berries accurately.

Winkle – Small shellfish in a dark grey, sharply pointed shell, common on rocks around the British coast.

Limpet – Flatter, larger shellfish that are common on rocky shores, found clinging to rocks.

Mussels – Mussels feed by filtering water, so only forage where you know the water to be clean. They have dark, elongated and asymmetrical shells, and are found attached to rocks on beaches. Steam the mussels to open them, and discard any that do not open through this process.

Hazelnuts – Hazel trees grow anywhere that isn't too damp, with nuts to be found from late August to October. The nuts are oval-shaped with a green husk.

Horseradish – The edible root of a plant with a white flower that blooms from May to September, common on waste ground.

Dewberry – Very similar to the blackberry in shape, though slightly smaller and purple to black in colour. Found in abundance in eastern England.

Bilberry – Widespread except in the south and east, this berry can be picked from July to September and is a greenish-pink sphere.

Elderflower – A deciduous shrub that has white flowers with five petals. These flowers themselves are edible, and have a cool, refreshing taste.

Laver – Edible seaweed found on the west coast of Britain. It can be boiled to make the Welsh dish laver bread, a purée traditionally eaten with cockles and bacon for breakfast, or used to create a soup or sauce. It is incredibly nutritious, containing iodine, protein and iron.

Marsh samphire – Common on salt marshes around the coast, this plant can be eaten either raw or cooked.

Mushrooms – Mushroom picking is an art form, and should not be undertaken lightly. Never eat a wild mushroom that has not been identified, and only eat a small amount if it is the first time you are trying a species.

Wild garlic – The garlic plant (*Allium ursinum*) grows close to, or amongst, bluebells. It has a strong smell of garlic and has long, green leaves which are the main usable part, great in soups and salads.

Dandelions – The dandelion is prevalent wherever things are growing, and flowers from February to November. All of the plant can be used; the leaves can be put into a salad, the roots can be ground to make coffee, and the flower petals made into dandelion wine.

Stinging nettles – As weeds, nettles grow in a wide variety of places. To remove the stinging quality, the nettle leaves must be soaked in water or cooked; when eaten they have a flavour similar to that of spinach.

'Marooned three years agone,' he continued, 'and lived on goats since then, and berries, and oysters. Wherever a man is, says I, a man can do for himself. But, mate, my heart is sore for Christian diet. You mightn't happen to have a piece of cheese about you, now? No? Well, many's the long night I've dreamed of cheese – toasted, mostly – and woke up again, and here I were.'

'If ever I can get aboard again,' said I, 'you shall have cheese by the stone.'

ROBERT LOUIS STEVENSON, *TREASURE ISLAND*

COOKS' TIPS – EATING AL FRESCO

- An umbrella will be handy at either end of the weather spectrum, keeping both you and your sandwiches dry on a wet day or protecting you from heatstroke and sunburn during more sunny times.

- Citronella candles will add to a romantic or calming atmosphere as well as repelling insects that may be after you.

- Food covers are useful for keeping away the aforementioned insects that may want a taste of your delicious meal.

- For something more formal than a picnic, bring a fold-up table, a tablecloth and some fold-up chairs with you.

- Bring wet wipes! If the food's good, someone is bound to get messy.

- Sitting in the sun can lead to dehydration, so make sure everybody has enough to drink.

- If possible, assemble sandwiches and wraps with moist fillings just before you eat, to prevent the bread becoming soggy.

- Chill your drinks the night before. This will ensure they're cold when you come to drink them and can also help keep food chilled.

- If the ground is likely to be wet, take a picnic blanket with a waterproof underside.

- Make sure your picnic basket is the right size for the amount of food you are taking with you: too big and it'll be unnecessarily cumbersome and your food may be squashed as the basket is moved around, too small and your food won't fit!

- Bring any implements you need with you. For example, if you have cans you will need a can opener and if you have bottles with a cork bring a corkscrew.

There is little more glorious, in summer, than sitting through hours of golden afternoons at a long wooden table with twelve or sixteen or twenty others, in winter warming limbs and souls with fires and food and wine.

VICTORIA COSFORD, *AMORE AND AMARETTI*

UNUSUAL COOKING METHODS

Pit cooking

This is a cooking technique that has been used for centuries and is still popular, and indeed essential, in many places around the world. In essence it is a natural slow cooker that can be as large or small as you like, meaning you can cook a meal as dainty as a chicken wing or as substantial as a whole pig.

The first task facing you is digging your pit; once that is done you need to line it with rocks or bricks and start building a fire on top. The fire needs to have burnt down to a layer of hot coals before you put the meat on and this will take a few hours at least so while it is burning you can prepare your meat. First, wrap it in numerous layers of foil or (if you want to be really authentic) layers of banana leaves, and then wrap the whole thing in some chicken wire to keep it all together and help you remove it from the pit when it is cooked.

When the fire is ready, place the meat in the pit and then cover it as quickly as possible with foliage and earth. It needs to be completely covered so the pit is starved of oxygen and therefore won't burn your meat. It's the hot coals that cook your meat, not fire.

Leave it for at least twelve hours but don't worry if you end up leaving it for longer – because the meat is tightly wrapped it won't dry out and can cope with a little overcooking.

Machine gun bacon

If you like your bacon cooked with a large dose of aggression and happen to have a 7.62-millimetre machine gun (minigun) lying around, this may be for you. Start by wrapping the barrel of your gun in tin foil and then again with your bacon, making sure you tie it all together with some string. Then wrap another layer of tin foil around the bacon, again tying it with string, and insert the barrel into the gun. You are now ready to go to war and cook your breakfast! If you like your bacon not too crispy, fire 150 rounds; 250 rounds should do it if you want it crispy.

Fried eggs

Being able to fry eggs on the pavement may be an urban myth but it is possible to start your day with a sizzling egg cooked on your car bonnet. For an egg to be fully cooked it needs to be heated at 70°C, a temperature that a car bonnet will rarely reach in Britain. However, in countries with hotter climates and low humidity it is perfectly possible to cook an egg on a car bonnet in about half an hour.

Lava cooking

On active volcanoes such as the Pacaya volcano in Guatemala, visitors can roast marshmallows over the stream of lava that flows down the side. The heat from the lava can also be used to cook larger items including whole pigs or chickens but it is not generally advised.

Manifold Destiny

In 1989 Bill Scheller, a travel writer, and Chris Maynard, a photographer, wrote a book called *Manifold Destiny* detailing the finer points of cooking on a car engine. It was whilst on a road trip from Montreal to Boston that the idea for the book was formed. They had heard stories of truckers keeping soup hot by placing it on their engines and decided to try it out with a package of smoked meat. After proving that it did indeed work they started to experiment with other foods and *Manifold Destiny* was born. In the book they provide cooking times in the form of miles (chicken will be cooked after 55 miles). The book has become something of a cult classic in American culinary circles.

MEAT MARKET

*The way you cut your meat
reflects the way you live.*

CONFUCIUS

WEIRD AND WONDERFUL MEAT RECIPES

Pressed duck – A traditional French dish, developed in the nineteenth century in the La Tour d'Argent restaurant in Paris. The duck is partially roasted and carved, and the remaining carcass is pressed to extract the blood and juices. This is then made into a sauce with the duck's liver and combined with the breast before serving.

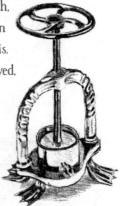

Turducken – A dish consisting of a deboned chicken stuffed into a deboned duck which itself is stuffed into a deboned turkey. Also rumoured to exist is the whole stuffed camel, which has varying ingredients including, in ascending order, fish, chicken, sheep and finally camel.

Ham in Coca-Cola – Gammon that has been boiled in Coca-Cola, then roasted. It gives the ham a sweet, spiky flavour and a lovely moist texture.

I want there to be no peasant in my kingdom so poor that he cannot have a chicken in his pot every Sunday.

HENRY IV OF FRANCE

If there is pure and elevated pleasure in this world, it is a roast pheasant with bread sauce.

SYDNEY SMITH

HAGGIS

The Scottish national dish: a sheep's liver, lung and heart minced with onion, oatmeal and spices, and cooked in the animal's stomach. The first written reference to the haggis is from the 1430 cookbook, *Liber Cure Cocorum*, as a dish called 'hagese' made of offal and herbs. In 2003, 33 per cent of American visitors to Scotland believed in the existence of the fictional animal, the wild haggis, from which the dish is supposedly made.

BLACK, WHITE AND RED PUDDING

British black pudding is made by soaking oatmeal in pork blood and forming it into a sausage. Versions of blood puddings have been served throughout history, such as by the Ancient Greeks and the Romans, and consequently there are different types of blood pudding all over Europe. British varieties include white pudding, which does not include blood but pork meat and fat, and red pudding, which includes various beef and pork products, and is deep-fried.

*The feeling of friendship is like that
of being comfortably filled with
roast beef; love, like being
enlivened with champagne.*

SAMUEL JOHNSON

My favourite animal is steak.

FRAN LEBOWITZ

*Life expectancy would grow by leaps
and bounds if green vegetables
smelled as good as bacon.*

DOUG LARSON

Soup from Kangaroo Tails

Ingredients: *1 tail, 2 lbs of beef, 3 carrots. 3 onions, a bunch of herbs, pepper and salt, butter.*

Mode: *Cut the tail into joints, and fry brown in butter; slice the vegetables and fry them also. Cut the meat into thin slices and boil all for four hours in 3 quarts of water. Take out the pieces of tail, strain the stock, thicken it with flour, put back the pieces of tail and boil another ten minutes before serving.*

Time: *4 to 5 hours*
Sufficient: *for 8 persons*
Seasonable in winter.

From *A Taste of the Past – Some Pioneer Cooks of Happy Valley and the Southern Hills*

Gently blow and stir the fire,
  Lay the mutton down to roast,
Dress it nicely I desire,
  In the dripping put a toast,
That I hunger may remove:
  Mutton is the meat I love.

On the dresser see it lie,
  Oh! the charming white and red!
Finer meat ne'er met my eye,
  On the sweetest grass it fed:
Let the jack go swiftly round,
  Let me have it nicely browned.

On the table spread the cloth,
  Let the knives be sharp and clean:
Pickles get and salad both,
  Let them each be fresh and green:
With small beer, good ale, and wine,
  O ye gods! how I shall dine.

JONATHAN SWIFT, 'HOW SHALL I DINE'

CALF'S HEAD

Take out the brains and boil the head, feet, and lights, in salted water, just enough to cover them, about two hours.

When they have boiled nearly an hour and a half, tie the brains in a cloth and put them in to boil with the rest.

They should be skinned, and soaked half an hour in cold water.

When the two hours have expired, take up the whole, and mash the brains fine, and season them with bread crumbs, pepper, salt, and a glass of Port or Claret, and use them for sauce.

Let the liquor remain for a soup the next day. It serves more handsomely to remove all the bones.

CATHERINE BEECHER, *MRS BEECHER'S RECEIPT-BOOK*

*I don't want any vegetables,
thank you. I paid for the
cow to eat them for me.*

DOUGLAS COUPLAND

Dear Lucy, you know what my wish is, –
  I hate all your Frenchified fuss:
Your silly entrées and made dishes
  Were never intended for us.
No footman in lace and in ruffles
  Need dangle behind my arm-chair,
And never mind seeking for truffles,
  Although they be ever so rare.

But a plain leg of mutton, my Lucy,
  I prithee get ready at three:
Have it smoking, and tender and juicy,
  And what better meat can there be?
And when it has feasted the master,
  'Twill amply suffice for the maid;
Meanwhile I will smoke my canaster,
  And tipple my ale in the shade.

WILLIAM MAKEPEACE THACKERAY, 'AD MINISTRAM'

COOKS' TIPS – WHAT A CARVE UP!

- ◉ Allow the meat standing time before carving. During this time it will finish cooking and will become easier to carve because as the meat cools, the muscles in it relax. This also keeps the meat juicy as relaxed muscle can hold more liquid.

- ◉ A carving fork for holding the meat steady and a sharp knife are essential.

- ◉ Ideally, carve the meat on a board with a groove round the outside to catch the juices. Avoid carving on anything like a dish, pan or platter as the raised edges will restrict the movement of your knife.

- ◉ Carve across the grain of the meat, and try to carve at the same angle for every slice.

- ◉ Cut dark meat before light meat as it will hold its moisture for a longer time.

- ◉ Have a heated serving plate, so your food will remain warm.

- ◉ Only carve what you will use to avoid leftover slices drying out before they are eaten.

- Be sure to save the juice from the dish the meat was cooked in, as this can be used to make a delicious gravy.

- If you are carving poultry, find out if it is a bird with any small bones that need to be removed before serving.

- If carving at the dinner table, make sure that any glasses or side plates are moved well out of the way.

Fruit and Veg

Vegetables are the food of the earth;
fruit seems more the food of the heavens.

SEPAL FELICIVANT

WHAT'S IN A NAME?

Loganberry – In 1883, Californian lawyer and horticulturist James Harvey Logan (1841–1928) accidentally crossed a blackberry and a raspberry, creating his eponymous fruit.

Caesar salad – Allegedly created at the Hotel Caesar in Tijuana Mexico in 1924 by Caesar Cardini, made up of the ingredients he had to hand when he was low on supplies, although a partner of Cardini, Paul Maggiora, claimed to have devised the salad in 1927 as the 'aviator's salad'. The dish consists of lettuce, croutons, parmesan cheese and a dressing of egg, lemon juice, olive oil and Worcestershire sauce.

The child who threw away leaf after leaf
of the many-coated onion, to get to
the sweet heart, found in the end that
he had thrown away the heart itself.

ALLEN UPWARD, 'THE ONION', FROM *SCENTED LEAVES FROM A CHINESE JAR*

*Parsley – the jewel of herbs, both
in the pot and on the plate.*

ALBERT STOCKLI

*The pleasures of taste to be derived from
a dinner of potatoes, beans, peas, turnips,
lettice, with a dessert of apples, gooseberries,
strawberries, currants, raspberries, and in
winter, oranges, apples and pears, is far
greater than is supposed.*

PERCY BYSSHE SHELLEY, 'A VINDICATION OF NATURAL DIET'

SAY IT WITH POTATOES –
TRY SOMETHING NEW

If you find yourself eating the same old things then stop being a *couch potato* and try something different. The *meat and potatoes* of it are that you will never create anything new if you don't try. Simply using a cookbook is *small potatoes*; you need to experiment with your own radical ideas. Your friends and family may think you are *half baked* when they see what you are doing. But when they try your food, your recipe could be the new *hot potato* – because everyone will want to pass it on.

HOW TO CARVE VEGETABLE GARNISHES

Rose carrot

- ◉ Cut the top off of a large carrot, giving it a flat end.

- ◉ In the centre of this surface, cut a 1-cm deep cone-shaped divot. This will end up being the centre of the flower.

- ◉ Divide the surface into five sections around the divot.

- ◉ With the point of a sharp knife, carve the first section into a petal, overlapping the next petal and so on around, making sure not to completely detach them.

- ◉ Finally, cut the whole flower off the carrot and neaten up the underside of the flower.

Courgette leaf

- ⊙ Cut a slice lengthways from a courgette. The side with the dark skin will be the area for creating the leaf pattern.

- ⊙ Trim this slice into the shape of a leaf.

- ⊙ Score the skin in two parallel lines lengthways down the slice to create the outline of a stem.

- ⊙ Cut triangles of skin pointing outwards from each of these lines, angled up towards the thin end of the leaf and becoming smaller towards the top of the leaf.

- ⊙ Finally, cut small triangles into the outside of the leaf.

Fried potatoes is a dish
Good as any one could wish:
Cheap it is, and appetizing;
Turn a saint to gormandizing:
Good and cheap and tasty too,
Just the thing for Love's Menu.

Love is dainty, and his food,
Even though common, must be good:
Love hath little to disburse,
So his fare must fit his purse:
Love hath fickle appetite,
We his palate must invite:
Crisp and hot, the price a sou,
Fried Potatoes, Love's Menu.

WILLIAM GAY, 'LOVE'S MENU POMMES DE TERRE FRITES'

Talking of Pleasure, this moment I was writing with one hand, and with thither holding to my Mouth a Nectarine – good God how fine. It went down soft pulpy, slushy, oozy – all its delicious embonpoint melted down my throat like a large Beatified Strawberry.

JOHN KEATS, LETTER TO CHARLES WENTWORTH DILKE,
22 SEPTEMBER 1818

CARROT JAM

Made with carrots chopped to fill a 1-litre bowl, three sliced lemons, one teaspoon of cinnamon, three cups of sugar and half a teaspoon of cloves. Simmer all ingredients in a saucepan for 20 minutes over a gentle heat.

Always eat grapes downwards – that is, always eat the best grape first; in this way there will be none better left on the bunch, and each grape will seem good down to the last. If you eat the other way, you will not have a good grape in the lot.

SAMUEL BUTLER, *THE NOTEBOOKS OF SAMUEL BUTLER*

Knock knock.
Who's there?
Lettuce.
Lettuce who?
Lettuce in and I'll tell you.

'Heavens! I was quite forgetting!' he cried suddenly. 'I have some wonderful raisins with me – you know, those seedless ones. Our new sutler has such first-rate things. I bought ten pounds. I always like sweet things. Will you have some?...' And Petya ran out to his Cossack in the passage and returned with baskets containing about five pounds of raisins. 'Help yourselves gentlemen, help yourselves!'

LEO TOLSTOY, *WAR AND PEACE*

ENERGY FOODS

Oats – High in potassium, calcium, vitamin E, vitamin B and much, much more. The perfect way to start the day.

Apricots – High in natural sugars, good for a quick boost of energy.

Broccoli – Full of fibre, vitamin A, vitamin C and has cancer-fighting properties (why mother always told you to eat your greens).

Spinach – High in antioxidants, folic acid, calcium and iron. All the better for fighting Bluto.

Banana – Great for either a quick burst of energy, or something to keep you going between meals. May also reduce the risk of certain types of cancer.

A nickel will get you on the subway, but garlic will get you a seat.

OLD NEW YORK PROVERB

Ready with leaves and with buds stood the tree.
'Shall I take them?' the frost said, now puffing with glee.
  'Oh my, no, let them stand,
  Till flowers are at hand!'
All trembling from tree-top to root came the plea.
Flowers unfolding the birds gladly sung.
'Shall I take them?' the wind said and merrily swung.
  'Oh my, no, let them stand,
  Till cherries are at hand!'
Protested the tree, while it quivering hung.
The cherries came forth 'neath the sun's glowing eye.
'Shall I take them?' a rosy young girl's eager cry.
  Oh my, yes, you can take,
  I've kept them for your sake!'
Low bending its branches, the tree brought them nigh.

BJØRNSTJERNE BJØRNSON, 'THE TREE'

Bottoms Up

When a recipe says 'add wine',
never ask 'To what?'

Anonymous

TYPES OF GLASSES

Collins glass – A tumbler, typically used to serve Tom Collins cocktails, which are made from gin, sugar, carbonated water and lemon juice.

Martini glass – A stemmed glass with a wide, cone-shaped bowl and a flat base. The stem is to avoid the drink being heated by the drinker's hand, and the wide bowl allows the drinker to enjoy the aroma.

Snifter – Also known as a balloon, with a short stem, a narrow top and wider bottom. This is traditionally used for drinks such as brandy and whisky, which benefit from being warmed by the drinker's hand.

Champagne flute – A stemmed glass with a tall, narrow bowl. The bowl shape is intended to allow the champagne to hold its carbonation by reducing the area at the surface.

Tulip glass – A glass intended for serving aromatic beers. It has a short stem, a bulbous bowl, and a flared rim which helps retain the head of the beer.

THERE is a rule to drink,
  I think,
A rule of three
That you'll agree
With me
Cannot be beat
And tends our lives to sweeten:
Drink ere you eat,
And while you eat,
And after you have eaten!

WALLACE RICE, 'A RULE OF THREE'

HOLY WATER

Dom Pérignon – A French Benedictine monk by the name of Dom Pierre Pérignon (1638–1715) is credited with creating the first real champagne by recognising the fact that certain grapes ferment twice, the second fermentation causing the fizz of champagne. Although well known as the inventor of the drink that is still synonymous with celebration to this day, it seems more likely that its real creator was the English physician and scientist Christopher Merret (1614/15–1695).

Westvleteren 'Trappist' beer – Made by Trappist monks to finance their monastery, this beer is one of only seven that can be called 'Trappist' and is considered by some to be the best beer in the world. The brewing of beer at the abbey of Saint Sixtus of Westvleteren began only seven years after it was opened in 1831.

Buckfast Tonic Wine – Buckfast Abbey, in Devon, is home to a Roman Catholic community of Benedictine monks who are known for creating a popular fortified wine since the end of the nineteenth century. In 1927 they lost their licence to sell wine but began working with wine merchants and changed the recipe to remove the tonic element. Due to its high alcohol and low price, the drink has become associated with anti-social behaviour and binge drinking, leading to calls for it to be banned.

Chartreuse – In the early seventeenth century, the Carthusian monks at a monastery in Vauvert, a suburb of Paris, received a gift of a manuscript detailing how to make a complex liqueur, an 'elixir of long life'. The manuscript was not properly translated for 100 years. In 1764 monks at the Grande Chartreuse monastery in Voiron, near Grenoble, adapted the recipe and the production of the green Chartreuse liqueur began in earnest. The potent drink (40 per cent alcohol) contains the extracts of over 130 plants and has a sweet yet spicy and pungent taste, and also comes in a milder, yellow version.

Hokey, pokey, whisky, thum,
How'd you like potatoes done?
Boiled in whisky, boiled in rum,
Says the King of the Cannibal Islands.

TRADITIONAL NURSERY RHYME

THE GIN CRAZE

The Gin Craze of the early eighteenth century followed the invasion and subsequent accession to the British throne of William of Orange in 1688–1689. Newly Protestant Britain was in conflict with Catholic France, and the government wanted to reduce trading with the French as much as possible so legislation was passed to limit import of French brandy and encourage gin production. As the turn of the century approached, more people were making gin, and subsequently it seemed that everyone was drinking it; even Queen Anne. What could only be described as an epidemic began, and the British government back-pedalled as fast as it could to slow the tide with restrictions on the production and sale of gin, which were widely ignored. The Gin Craze was only stopped by a combination of more even-handed legislation and a series of poor harvests which lead to reduced income for the masses. But it was immortalised by William Hogarth's prints, *Beer Street* and *Gin Lane* (1751), depicting the dangers of gin drinking contrasted with the more innocent pleasures of beer.

Some weasel took the cork out of my lunch.

W. C. FIELDS

Wine is the intellectual part of a meal while meat is the material.

ALEXANDRE DUMAS

HANGOVER CURES

Fry-up – The sausages and bacon contain calories to boost your energy. They also contain amino acid, as do the eggs, which helps to clear the toxins out of your body. If a whole fry-up is too much, the bread in a bacon sandwich speeds up the metabolism and gets rid of the alcohol. Some swear by raw egg, or having milk or fatty sausage before drinking.

Sour milk – In Poland, sour pickle juice or sour milk is used. Simply leave a pint of milk out at room temperature before you go drinking. The next morning down the lot and see if it works.

Hair of the dog – It might feel like the worst idea in the world but science (supposedly) suggests that it may make you feel better, if only for a short time. A favourite, which may also contain some goodness, is the Bloody Mary, a cocktail consisting of vodka and tomato juice.

Tripe soup – A Romanian soup made from cow stomach. Add some vegetables, vinegar and cream and the resulting greasy, salty concoction is the perfect cure for a sore head (or enough to put you off getting one in the first place).

TEATIME

There are few hours in life more agreeable than the hour dedicated to the ceremony known as afternoon tea.

HENRY JAMES

COOKS' TIPS – THE PERFECT CUPPA

George Orwell had 'Eleven Golden Rules for Making Tea', such as using a ceramic teapot, tea from India or Ceylon (Sri Lanka), warming the pot, using six spoonfuls of leaves per litre and taking the teapot to the kettle so the water will still be boiling when you pour it in. Here are a few more from the aficionados:

⊙ Whether in a cup or pot, always brew tea for at least five minutes.

⊙ After the tea is made and the milk is added, leave to stand for five minutes before drinking.

⊙ To get the true taste of tea, do not use sugar.

Tea to the English is really a picnic indoors.

ALICE WALKER

If man has no tea in him, he is incapable of understanding truth and beauty.

JAPANESE PROVERB

TEA FACTS

- ◉ After water, tea is the most widely consumed beverage in the world. More tea is consumed than alcohol, soft drinks, hot chocolate and coffee combined.

- ◉ China produces the most tea per country, creating 1,375,780 tonnes in 2009.

- ◉ In Chinese legend, tea was discovered by Emperor Shennong, when leaves from a tree were blown into his boiling water.

- ◉ Tea was introduced to the British court in the 1660s by the wife of King Charles II, Portuguese princess Catherine of Braganza, from where it spread to the bourgeoisie and the country as a whole.

- ◉ In Britain, 66 per cent of the population drink tea every day, and 98 per cent of them take milk in their tea, while 96 per cent is made from teabags.

- ◉ Various types of tea have been said to boost mental alertness and the immune system, counteract bad breath, reduce the risk of a stroke, treat abscesses and tumours and lower the risk of cardiovascular disease.

- ◉ The Mad Hatter first appears in Lewis Carroll's novel *Alice's Adventures in Wonderland*. Time has stopped for the Hatter, meaning it is constantly 6 p.m. for him, or 'Teatime!'

The first cup moistens my lips and throat,
The second cup breaks my loneliness,
The third cup searches my barren entrail
but to find therein some five thousand
    volumes of odd ideographs.
The fourth cup raises a slight perspiration, –
All the wrong of life passes away through my
    pores.
At the fifth cup I am purified;
The sixth cup calls me to the realms of
    immortals.
The seventh cup – ah, but I
could take no more! I only feel
the breath of cool wind that rises
    in my sleeves.
Where is Horaisan?
Let me ride on this sweet breeze
And waft away thither.

LO TUNG, 'CUPS OF TEA'

FINEST EARL GREY TEA

Charles Grey, British Prime Minister from 1830 to 1834 and the second Earl Grey, supposedly received a gift of the tea, which was originally Chinese, and passed on the recipe to Jacksons of Piccadilly, who first produced it commercially as Earl Grey tea. Its distinctive flavour comes from the bergamot oil (extracted from the fragrant rind of the bergamot orange) which is added to the leaves.

Where there's tea there's hope.

ARTHUR W. PINERO

Tea is one of the mainstays of civilisation in this country.

GEORGE ORWELL

CLASSIC TEATIME TREATS

Rock cake – A fruit cake named for its rough and rocky surface, the earliest known recipe for rock cake comes from the 1860s, when it included lemon and brandy. The baking of rock cakes in lieu of regular cakes was encouraged during World War Two as rock cakes use less sugar and eggs.

Scone – A type of cake made with baking powder, the scone can be savoury or sweet, possibly including either dried fruit or cheese. The sweet variant is a vital ingredient to a cream tea, which is tea (the drink), served with scones, cream and jam. There is much debate over the correct pronunciation of the word, some pronouncing it to rhyme with 'cone', some with 'con'.

Muffins – Not to be confused with the sweet American cupcake-shaped muffin. The name comes from either the German plural for soft cake, *Muffen*, or the Old French *moufflet*, a word used to describe bread as soft. Muffin men, who delivered muffins, were immortalised in the nineteenth-century nursery rhyme which begins, 'Do you know the muffin man?' They are typically served cut in half, toasted and buttered, and sometimes filled with meat or egg as a breakfast sandwich.

Jam tarts – Tarts were introduced to Britain in medieval times, the name coming from Old French. The jam tart consists of a simple pastry case filled with jam, and due to its simplicity is one of the first things that people learn to cook as children.

Sally Lunn bun – This is a type of yeast bread purported to be named after a French immigrant to Bath in 1680. The story of Sally Lunn (originally named Solange Luyon) was discovered in the mid 1930s, when the current resident of her house found documents in her home detailing the recipe and its background. However, the papers were lost by their discoverer, prompting the question of whether the story was a fabrication.

Chorus:

Now to the banquet we press;
  Now for the eggs, the ham,
Now for the mustard and cress,
  Now for the strawberry jam!
Now for the tea of our host,
  Now for the rollicking bun,
Now for the muffin and toast,
  Now for the gay Sally Lunn!

Women: The eggs, and the ham, and the strawberry jam!
Men: The rollicking bun, and the gay Sally Lunn!
  The rollicking, rollicking bun!

WILLIAM SCHWENCK GILBERT, *THE SORCERER*

THE FOOD OF LOVE

Cooking is like love. It should be entered into with abandon or not at all.

HARRIET VAN HORNE

MOUTH-WATERING MOMENTS
ON THE SILVER SCREEN

Chocolat – Starring Juliette Binoche and Johnny Depp, this film tells the story of a young mother who opens a *chocolaterie* in a small French town and the effect she, and her chocolate, have on the townspeople.

Lady and the Tramp – Disney's tale of the romance between two dogs includes the famous, much parodied scene in which Lady and the Tramp share a candlelit dinner outside an Italian restaurant.

Babette's Feast – A Danish film directed by Gabriel Axel, *Babette's Feast* tells the story of a woman fleeing counter-revolutionary violence in Paris, who takes on the role of housekeeper to two sisters who manage a congregation in the countryside. The woman, Babette, wins the lottery and offers to create a magnificent feast, and in doing so reinvigorates them spiritually and physically.

The Cook, the Thief, His Wife & Her Lover – A romantic crime drama starring Michael Gambon and Helen Mirren, directed by Peter Greenaway. The film tells the story of a restaurant taken over by a gangster (Gambon) whose wife (Mirren) begins an affair with a patron. Eventually, the couple are found out, with disastrous and unusual culinary results.

Tom Jones – The 1963 adaptation of one of the first books to be considered a novel contains a memorable dinner scene. Tom Jones is having dinner at an inn with Mrs Waters, whom he has recently saved from a redcoat officer. They gorge themselves on a huge feast including soup, beer, bread, chicken, beef, lobster and oysters whilst lustily gazing at one another across the table.

I know that out-of-date pasta is hardly a reason for splitting up with someone. But in my mind, food and love are very closely linked – I go to a huge effort to prepare meals for friends and people that I care about – and it seemed like a message of sorts.

KAREN WHEELER, *TOUTE ALLURE*

TEN GREAT FOOD SONGS

1. 'Let's Call the Whole Thing Off'
   Fred Astaire and Ginger Rogers
2. 'Do You Love Me'
   The Contours
3. 'The Onion Song'
   Marvin Gaye and Tammi Terrell
4. 'My Boy Lollipop'
   Millie Small
5. 'I Want Candy'
   The Strangeloves
6. 'On the Good Ship Lollipop'
   Shirley Temple
7. 'Peaches'
   The Presidents of the United States of America
8. 'Green Onions'
   Booker T. and the M.G.s
9. 'If I Knew You Were Comin' I'd've Baked a Cake'
   Eileen Barton
10. 'Yes! We Have No Bananas'
    Billy Jones

With strawberries we filled a tray,
And then we drove away, away
  Along the links beside the sea,
  Where wave and wind were light and free,
And August felt as fresh as May.

And where the springy turf was gay
With thyme and balm and many a spray
  Of wild roses, you tempted me
  With strawberries!

A shadowy sail, silent and gray,
Stole like a ghost across the bay;
  But none could hear me ask my fee,
  And none could know what came to be.
Can sweethearts all their thirst allay
  With strawberries?

WILLIAM ERNEST HENLEY, 'WITH STRAWBERRIES'

FOOD FOR SEDUCTION

Aniseed – Used greatly by the ancient Greeks and Romans, aniseed contains oestrogenic compounds (oestrogen being the female sex hormone), which have a similar effect to testosterone and affect both genders.

Bananas – Contain potassium and vitamin B, chemicals that improve the production of sex hormones.

Chocolate – Cocoa beans contain phenethylamine, a chemical which causes the brain to release endorphins, neurotransmitters that are produced during pleasure, love, excitement, etc.

Garlic – Increases circulation and is a mild stimulant.

Honey – It was traditional in Europe to give a newly married couple enough mead for a month to encourage happiness and fertility, hence the word 'honeymoon'.

Lettuce – Considered by the Ancient Egyptians to be an aphrodisiac, though the Ancient Greeks found it to be a sedative due to the chemical lactucin.

Oysters – Casanova is said to have eaten fifty oysters every morning with his mistress of the time, and they have long been reputed to have an aphrodisiac quality. Researchers have found that oysters do have high levels of rare amino acids, which increase the level of sex hormone in the body.

There are few virtues a man can possess more erotic than culinary skill.

ISABEL ALLENDE

Food, Beauty-ful Food

Egg white mask – Simply apply one egg white, beaten until smooth, to your face, let it dry completely then rinse off. Refreshing and tautening.

Lemon juice hair lightener – Combine the juice of half a lemon with a handful of leave-in conditioner. Apply to hair, comb through and wash out.

Olive oil moisturiser – Use in small doses as massage oil or a daily lotion.

Pumpkin pedicure – Combine half a cup of pumpkin purée with one egg and apply to your feet and calves. After 15–20 minutes, rinse off with warm water.

Avocado face mask – Apply a whole mashed avocado to your face and wash off after three minutes to treat dry skin.

Vodka astringent – To cleanse and tighten your pores, rub vodka-soaked cotton wool on your face.

Mayonnaise conditioner – Apply the mayonnaise to hair like a normal conditioner, leave in for fifteen minutes and rinse hair twice.

Beer hair treatment – To increase the shine and volume of your hair, pour a whole can of beer onto clean hair, massage it in, then rinse.

Comfort Food

Lancashire hotpot – The archetypal pub dish, consisting of lamb or mutton and onion topped with sliced potatoes and cooked in a casserole dish for a very, very long time. Eternally associated with Betty at the Rovers Return pub in *Coronation Street.*

Rice pudding – There are many types of rice pudding around the world, but it has existed in Britain since Tudor times in one form or another. It can be made from scratch, but for the true memory of youth, canned rice pudding is always best.

Tomato soup – Not cold gazpacho, not chunky, and definitely NOT powdered. From a can, a warming pick-me-up just when you need it.

Roast dinner – Traditionally served on a Sunday, very few things compare to the home comfort felt when eating a roast dinner with all its accompaniments.

Fish and chips – A firm favourite with the British working class for over a century, fried fish was allegedly introduced to Britain by Jewish immigrants from Portugal and Spain. The first fish and chip shop opened in London in 1860.

Chocolate – Generally viewed as a more feminine comfort food, yet enjoyed by all regardless, being included in ration packs for both the US and UK armed forces. Contains a variety of substances that are associated with pleasure in human physiology.

Kissing don't last: cookery do.

GEORGE MEREDITH

BEST OF BRITISH

Ask not what you can do for your country.
Ask what's for lunch.

ORSON WELLES

So are you to my thoughts as food to life,
Or as sweet-season'd showers are to the ground;
And for the peace of you I hold such strife
As 'twixt a miser and his wealth is found;
Now proud as an enjoyer and anon
Doubting the filching age will steal his treasure,
Now counting best to be with you alone,
Then better'd that the world may see my pleasure;
Sometime all full with feasting on your sight
And by and by clean starved for a look;
Possessing or pursuing no delight,
Save what is had or must from you be took.
Thus do I pine and surfeit day by day,
Or gluttoning on all, or all away.

WILLIAM SHAKESPEARE, 'SONNET 75'

BRITAIN ON A PLATE

The UK may be a small country but it boasts a vast variety of foods, accents and cultures across its different regions. British cuisine is now a melting pot of worldwide influences but some traditional regional dishes remain and prosper. After a lull in the reputation of British food during the 1960s and 1970s, things have taken a turn for the better, as British restaurants and celebrity chefs have gained worldwide recognition. Our regional foods are also flourishing, amidst protection legislation from the European courts and the rise and rise of local farmers' markets.

Melton Mowbray pork pie – The pork pies made in this Leicestershire town became popular with local huntsmen in the nineteenth century, and their fame spread throughout the country with the arrival of the railways. An authentic Melton Mowbray pie is made from hand-raised pastry, filled with the finest fresh (uncured) pork, topped up with bone-stock jelly and wrapped in parchment.

Bury black pudding – Although many would quail at the thought of pigs' blood for breakfast, when mixed with oatmeal in a sausage and fried or grilled in slices it becomes a classic part of the Full English. In Bury, one of the heartlands of the black pudding, it's a popular takeaway snack, boiled and served in brown paper with lashings of malt vinegar.

Yorkshire pudding – One of the quintessential components of a roast dinner is the Yorkshire pudding. It is the perfect accompaniment to England's national dish of roast beef, although it is often served with lamb, chicken and pork, too. The history of the dish is unclear. The first recorded mention is in the book *The Whole Duty of a Woman* in 1737 where the recipe for *a dripping pudding* is given, but the true origins of the Yorkshire pudding are shrouded in mystery and it is likely the world will never learn the truth. (It doesn't have to be from Yorkshire to be called a Yorkshire pudding but who knows if that could change in the future.)

FOODS INVENTED IN THE UK

E very country or region has contributed in some way towards the cuisine of planet earth. The Italians gave us pizza, sushi derives from Japan, and the Americans claim hamburgers (though people were eating these in Britain before the USA existed). It is often difficult to know where a food was first made but there are a few that the British can certainly hold their hands up to and say 'this is ours'.

Marmite – Invented in 1902 in Burton-on-Trent, it is the infamous 'love it or hate it' food. Created from yeast extract, a by-product of beer brewing, it is dark brown, savoury, salty and delicious/disgusting. It is commonly spread on bread and toast or thrown in the bin. Is it is often mistaken by tourists for shoe polish.

HP Sauce – Invented in 1895 by Frederick Gibson Garton from Nottingham, HP Sauce is now the most popular brown sauce in the UK. The HP stands for Houses of Parliament; Garton had been told that the sauce was being served to MPs in the parliament restaurant. The sauce is now popular in Canada and the United States and comes in a number of varieties.

The sandwich – It is impossible to say when someone first placed a meat or vegetable substance inside two pieces of bread and ate it. What it is possible to say is that this method of food preparation is now universally known as the sandwich and that is a term that first originated in the UK in 1762. John Montagu, the 4th Earl of Sandwich, is the man whose name is uttered at lunchtime everyday. His friends observed with interest when he ordered some meat in between two pieces of bread in order to keep his hands clean when playing cards and began to do the same. So 'I'll have one of those things the Earl of Sandwich has' became 'a sandwich'.

Worcestershire sauce – Invented in 1837 on Broad Street, Worcester, by two chemists, John Wheeley Lea and William Henry Perrins, it is regarded as a condiment. The sauce is rumoured to originate from an Indian curry powder recipe that was given to them. They then made the powder into a solution but on tasting it discovered it was far too strong, so they relegated the barrel to the basement. Three years later, out of curiosity they opened the barrel, found it had fermented and tasted it anew. The result is what we use today. There are now many varieties and brands of Worcester sauce in the UK and abroad. Worcester and Worcestershire (two and three syllables) are both acceptable forms of pronunciation.

FAMOUS BRITISH COOKS

King Alfred

According to legend, whilst fleeing from the invading Danish army in 878, King Alfred came across a small house in the woods. In search of rest and food, he entered. The peasant woman inside offered to help the unknown stranger and asked him to watch some cakes she was cooking on the fire. His mind being preoccupied, Alfred let the cakes burn and the woman scolded him for his absent-mindedness. If the only English monarch still known as 'the Great' can make such a mistake, then it can surely be forgiven in the rest of us!

Mrs Beeton

Mrs Beeton's Book of Household Management, as the title suggests, was not just a cookbook; it gave advice on many aspects of housekeeping. It did, however, dedicate 900 of its 1,112 pages to recipes, so it is often known as *Mrs Beeton's Cookbook*. It was the first cookbook to list the ingredients at the beginning of the recipe in the way cookbooks do today. It was also an immediate best-seller and continues to sell, with many British households owning a copy. It gives a great insight into how the Victorians viewed household management and can be seen as one of the first modern cookbooks.

Elizabeth David

Somewhat of a renegade her whole life, Elizabeth David (1913–1992) revolutionised cooking in Britain in the twentieth century. She was an art student, an actress, a librarian then a cooking writer. She first brought Mediterranean cookery to Britain when she returned from Cairo after the war, having travelled the Mediterranean and fallen in love with its food, becoming particularly fond of French cooking. She soon became dismayed at the bland nature of cooking back home. All her books had a huge impact on British cooking but it is *French Provincial Cooking* that is probably her most famous publication. It is written with personality and extensive knowledge and much of our modern cuisine can be traced back to this book. A lot of books may claim to have had a profound influence on a culture or society – this one truly did. She introduced olive oil, garlic, basil, red and green peppers and aubergine into the everyday lexicon of British cooks.

Fanny Cradock

Fanny Cradock (1909–1994) was born Phyllis Nan Sortain Pechey, and her food career began when she started working at various restaurants around London. This led to a column she co-wrote with her partner, Johnnie, for *The Daily Telegraph*. From the success of this they moved on to a career in theatre, in which their act would be accompanied by dinner served to the audience. Fanny's rise to fame continued when the BBC commissioned a cookery show, *Fanny's Kitchen*. She introduced extravagant-looking yet cost-effective food to the homes of 1950s Britain, and is remembered as much for her flamboyant cooking as her extrovert nature.

TASTY TITBITS

*'Tis an ill cook that cannot
lick his own fingers.*

WILLIAM SHAKESPEARE, *ROMEO AND JULIET*

COFFEE FACTS

- ◉ The coffee plant, of the *Coffea* genus, is native to southern Asia and subtropical Africa.

- ◉ Decaffeinated coffee was first created commercially in 1903 by Ludwig Roselius and Karl Wimmer, German coffee merchants.

- ◉ In 2009, Brazil produced the most coffee beans per country worldwide, producing a total of 2,440,060 tonnes.

- ◉ In South America, instant coffee is preferred over fresh.

- ◉ Finland is the largest consumer of coffee per capita, consuming 12 kilograms per person in 2008.

- ◉ In 1511, coffee was forbidden by orthodox imams in Mecca; however, this was overturned by Sultan Selim I of the Ottoman Empire and Grand Mufti Mehmet Ebussuud el-Imadi.

- ◉ Moderate coffee drinking can reduce the risk of Alzheimer's and Parkinson's disease, liver disease, certain types of cancer and enhances the effects of analgesics.

Coffee smells like freshly ground heaven.

JESSI LANE ADAMS

*Decaffeinated coffee is kind
of like kissing your sister.*

BOB IRWIN

*Coffee makes us severe,
and grave, and philosophical.*

JONATHAN SWIFT

COOKING THE BOOKS –
SOME FAMOUS COOKBOOKS

Larousse Gastronomique

Larousse Gastronomique is not a cookbook as such, it is an encyclopaedia of gastronomy. The first edition was edited by Prosper Montagné in 1938 and since then numerous editions have been published and it continues to sell in large numbers. It predominantly deals with French cuisine but over the years lots of non-French recipes have been added. It is a must-have book for any chef.

Len Deighton's Action Cook Book

Len Deighton has written successful novels, been a graphic designer, newspaper columnist, film producer and he wrote the world famous *Len Deighton's Action Cook Book*, designed for the bachelor who wants to know his way around a kitchen. It provides far more than the usual collection of recipes, giving advice on what wines go with what foods, what kitchen equipment to buy and even details about the science of cooking. Some of the recipes may seem a little dated but it will still provide the inspiration for any man who wants to take up cooking.

The Alice B. Toklas Cook Book

An American emigrant to Paris at the beginning of the twentieth century, on arriving in Paris Toklas quickly encountered Gertrude

Stein, an American writer, poet and art collector, and became her life partner. Following the publication of *The Autobiography of Alice B. Toklas*, actually written by Stein, Toklas was reluctant to write her own memoirs so wrote a combined memoir and cookbook. The most famous recipe included is for 'Hashish Fudge', or cannabis brownies.

The Forme of Cury

This extensive recipe collection from the fourteenth century was written by 'the master cooks of Richard II'. It was originally written in Middle English and contains around 200 recipes. It is one of the oldest known sets of cooking instructions in the English language, and contains both everyday dishes and more extravagant creations.

Mastering the Art of French Cooking

Julia Child (1912–2004) moved to Paris with her husband after World War Two, and found French cuisine to be a revelation. There, she studied French cooking extensively and eventually began to teach others, her famous book making French cooking accessible to Americans in the early 1960s. She began appearing on television, quickly becoming extremely popular, and continued to cook on television and write cookery books for the next forty years.

*Food is a massive memory trigger,
and it strikes me that sausages
are pretty bad offenders. Just ask
anyone who lived through the
Second World War in Britain about
sawdust bangers; on the other hand,
don't we all have at least one great
hot dog moment in our lives?*

JOHN BARLOW, *EVERYTHING BUT THE SQUEAL*

LIFE'S MORE UNUSUAL SAUSAGE FILLINGS

Eighty-eight per cent of sausages are made from pork but there are probably not many meats that, at some point, haven't been made into a sausage. The whole idea of a sausage lends itself to creativity and experimentation – you can basically put in whatever you want! Here are a few sausages that you may take a second glance at if you notice them in your local butchers:

- Ostrich, brandy, sage and parsley
- Pheasant and whisky
- Smoked beer and beef
- Pork, banana and honey
- Pork, chilli and chocolate
- Pork, vodka, tomato and Worcestershire sauce
- Pork and maple syrup
- Irn-Bru

CURRYWURST

Germany is famous for a number of its sausages but the most popular in Germany itself is the currywurst; hot pork sausage cut into slices and served with a curry sauce. The sauce is often made from ketchup or tomato paste mixed with large amounts of curry powder.

It was first made in Berlin in 1949 by Herta Heuwer who had been alerted to the delights of tomato ketchup, Worcestershire sauce and curry powder by British soldiers. She decided to combine these ingredients to make a sauce which she poured over grilled sausage and started selling on a street stand in the Charlottenburg district. It soon became so popular that Herta was selling 10,000 portions a week, persuading her to patent the sauce in 1951, calling it 'Chillup'.

Over the years currywurst has become a symbol of German popular culture, even having its rise to fame charted in a novel and film. *Die Entdeckung der Currywurst* (The Discovery of the Currywurst) was written by Uwe Timm and later adapted into a film of the same name. The plot follows an alternative and as yet unproven theory that currywurst was first created in Hamburg

WHAT'S IN A NAME?

Beef Wellington – This dish of beef steak cooked in pastry was possibly named for the 1st Duke of Wellington, Arthur Wellesley (1769–1852). Some believe his personal chef invented it for him; others simply point out that the dish has a remarkable similarity to the duke's eponymous boot (in shape, not taste, of course!).

Pizza Margherita – Named in honour of Queen Margherita of Savoy (1851–1926). On a visit to Naples c. 1889, she was presented a pizza representing the colours of the Italian flag: white (mozzarella), green (basil) and red (tomato).

KEY DATES – THE NINETEENTH CENTURY

1810 – The first canned food was invented by Frenchman Nicolas Appert.

1823 – The first grapefruit tree was planted in Florida. The American state now produces more grapefruits than the rest of the world combined.

1826 – Wholemeal bread was discovered to be healthier than the white bread eaten by the rich.

1837 – Chemists John Wheeley Lea and William Henry Perrins created Worcestershire sauce.

1847 – The first chocolate bar was made by Fry's in Bristol.

1868 – Tabasco sauce was invented by Edmund McIlhenny in Louisiana.

1891 – The first electric kettle was developed.

1895 – Frederick Gibson Garton, a Nottingham grocer, created HP Sauce.

1886 – Coca-Cola was developed.

1896 – Heinz opened its first office in the UK.

Key Dates – 1900–1950

1902 – Marmite was first sold in England.

1904 – Thomas Sullivan invented the teabag in New York City.

1913 – Wall's began making and selling ice cream as well as meat.

1927 – There was pie in the sky as Imperial Airways served the first hot airline meals.

1928 – Harry Ramsden opened the first sit down fish and chip restaurant.

1929 – Bib-Label Lithiated Lemon-Lime Soda was invented (better known as 7UP).

1930 – Sliced bread first sold in England and instantly became the best thing...

1937 – Milk was handed out for free in all schools.

1939 – Instant coffee appeared on the shelves and mornings became easier.

1948 – The first ever McDonald's was opened.

KEY DATES - 1950-2000

1952 – The first espresso machine was produced.

1954 – Rationing in the UK ended.

1965 – The first Pizza Express restaurant opened in London.

1974 – The first domestic microwave oven went on sale.

1979 – Free milk stopped being handed out in schools.

1987 – Red Bull was first created and sold in Austria.

1988 – UK egg sales fell by 10 per cent as Edwina Currie claimed most British eggs were infected with salmonella.

1990 – Conservative MP John Gummer fed a beef burger to his daughter in an attempt to convince people that British beef was safe from BSE.

1996 – Tesco became the first supermarket to offer online shopping.

KEY DATES - 2000 ONWARDS

2000 - The UK Food Standards Agency was opened. Its purpose was to protect the British public in relation to food.

2001 - Foot-and-mouth disease struck in the UK - apocalypse cow!

2002 - US President George W. Bush choked on a pretzel and fainted at the White House.

2005 - The European Court of Justice confirmed that all cheese sold as feta must originate from Greece.

2007 - After his appearance on *Dragon's Den*, Levi Roots's Reggae Reggae Sauce went on sale nationwide in the UK.

The square is now filled with the smell of food: the scent of sugar and vanilla from a stand busily selling crêpes and warm, spicy apple juice is superseded by the aroma of fried onions and sausages from a neighbouring marchand as we walk around the market.

KAREN WHEELER, *TOUT SWEET*

Food for Thought

Oregano is the spice of life.

Henry J. Tillman

Worries go down better with soup.

JEWISH PROVERB

All happiness depends on a leisurely breakfast.

JOHN GUNTHER

Undue significance a starving man attaches
To food
Far off; he sighs, and therefore hopeless,
And therefore good.

Partaken, it relieves indeed, but proves us
That spices fly
In the receipt. It was the distance
Was savoury.

EMILY DICKINSON, 'UNDUE SIGNIFICANCE A STARVING MAN ATTACHES'

*After a good dinner, one can forgive
anybody, even one's relatives.*

OSCAR WILDE

*Strange to see how a good dinner
and feasting reconciles everybody.*

SAMUEL PEPYS

Life is too short, and I'm Italian. I'd much rather eat pasta and drink wine than be a size zero.

SOPHIA BUSH

Life is a combination of magic and pasta.

FEDERICO FELLINI

*What does cooking mean?... It means...
knowledge of all herbs, and fruits and balms
and spices... It means carefulness, inventiveness,
and watchfulness... It means much testing and
no wasting... It means English thoroughness
and French art and Arabian hospitality.*

John Ruskin

*The menu, like the guest list, was a mixture
of new friends and old favourites...*

Elizabeth Bard, *Lunch in Paris*

*If hunger makes you irritable,
better eat and be pleasant.*

JUDAH BEN SAMUEL, *SEFER HASIDIM*

*Food to Galicians was a symbol of celebration
in tough times, a respite against hardship. And
the more food, the greater the celebration.*

JOHN BARLOW, *EVERYTHING BUT THE SQUEAL*

... the reason I should work hard, create magnificent food and always do my best is not a needy search for approval and praise, but because it is a worthy way to live.

VICTORIA COSFORD, *AMORE AND AMARETTI*

Beautiful soup, so rich and green,
Waiting in a hot tureen!
Who for such dainties would not stoop?
Soup of the evening, beautiful Soup!

Soup of the evening, beautiful Soup!
Beau-ootiful Soo-oop! Beau-ootiful Soo-oop!
Soo-oop of the e-e-evening, Beautiful, beautiful Soup

LEWIS CARROLL, 'THE MOCK TURTLE'S SONG'

HUNGRY FOR BLOGS

Tell me what you eat, and I will tell you what you are.

JEAN-ANTHELME BRILLAT-SAVARIN

If you love food then the Internet is a fantastic resource, teeming with people who also love food and are generous enough to share their passion and expertise with the world. Here are some brilliant food blogs that will leave you inspired and hungry!

Scrambling Eggs

http://www.scramblingeggs.blogspot.com

Written by a London cafe owner, this blog is light-hearted and entertaining. It combines tasty recipes with the pleasures of owning a London cafe.

Coco and Me

http://www.cocoandme.com

If you are craving something sweet then be warned: this blog may drive you to insanity! It is filled with cake and chocolate recipes along with plenty of photos.

Bangers and Sausages

http://bangersandsausages.blogspot.com

If you really love sausages then check out this site for loads of sausage reviews and interesting recipe ideas.

The Lambshank Redemption

http://thelambshankredemption.blogspot.com

This is written by a freelance food journalist and is similar to a regular food column. It contains reviews of food from all over the world from a man who can certainly eat!

Orangette
http://orangette.blogspot.com

Honest and readable, this blog contains a lot of personality from the writer so you can discover how food impacts on her everyday life. It's easy to become hooked on this blog!

Matt Bites
http://mattbites.com

May leave you a little unsure of the distinction between art and food. Matt Bites is a professional photographer and this blog is packed with some fantastic images.

The Pioneer Woman
http://thepioneerwoman.com/cooking

Brilliant home-on-the-range type cooking, including a recipe for pork cooked in Dr Pepper! Uses a lot of photos, which makes the recipes so much easier to follow.

Gluten Free Girl and the Chef
http://glutenfreegirl.com

She proves that gluten free food can be exciting and provides a heart-warming personal tale intertwined with great recipes.

Delicious Days

http://www.deliciousdays.com

Everything a food blog should be; great recipes for fantastic food.

Culinary Travels

http://culinarytravels.co.uk

A blogger who is passionate about eating food sourced as locally as possible, offering recipes, reviews, articles and various musings on food and cooking in general.

the handyface blog

http://handyface.wordpress.com

A man named Andy is attempting to return the art of cheese making to the kitchens of Britain. A great resource to find out what you need and how to make your own.

Lunch in Paris and Provence

http://www.elizabethbard.com

Author of the international bestseller Lunch in Paris, Elizabeth Bard moved to Provence and provides luscious photos with her personal recipes of such seasonal food as cherry clafoutis, as well as tips for mums with small children.

VEGETARIAN/VEGAN BLOGS

The Lazy Vegetarian

http://thelazyvegetarian.blogspot.com

Quick and easy vegetarian recipes abound on this blog, with a log of what the family ate that week, and reviews of various meat substitutes, such as vegetarian sausages.

Veggie Belly

http://www.veggiebelly.com

This recipe blog from an Indian-American in Virginia focuses on Indian cuisine, but also includes Brazilian, Mexican and Middle Eastern dishes. World vegetarian cooking at its best.

Vegan Kingdom

http://vegankingdom.co.uk

This UK-based blogger posts various vegan recipes, as well as reviews of vegan and raw food products, distributors and restaurants.

FORAGING BLOGS

Fat of the Land

http://fat-of-the-land.blogspot.com

From Seattle, Langdon Cook uses foraging as a way to reconnect with the land and includes stories and tips on the foraging and cooking of clams, fish, mushrooms, truffles, oyster, squid and plants such as dandelions and stinging nettles, as well as discussing the environmental issues and the effects of the modern world on foraging.

The Mushroom Diary

http://www.mushroomdiary.co.uk

In this blog, amateur mushroom hunter John Harris of Leicestershire details the edible and inedible mushrooms he finds, sharing information and tips.

Wild Food, Mushrooms and Fishing

http://wildfoodmushroomsfishing.blogspot.com

This blogger from Essex provides recipes for everything from Wild Rose Petal Jam Roly-Poly to Stinging Nettle and Potato Soup, and the occasional introduction to various plants, seafood, mushrooms – anything you can forage!

RESTAURANT REVIEW BLOGS

London Eater

http://londoneater.com

Restaurant reviews of London, and occasionally beyond, by Kang Leong. Each review is accompanied by his beautiful photography, and generally covers the higher end of the capital's restaurants.

Food Snob

http://foodsnobblog.wordpress.com/

He reviews some of the finest restaurants in the world in such detail that you really start to believe you're there.

Passport Delicious

http://www.passportdelicious.com

A blog run by Atlantic-hopping Krista, who currently resides in Chicago but started her blog when she was living in London. The blog includes restaurant reviews from both cities, as well as the occasional hotel review, all done in a casual, humorous tone.

eggbaconchipsandbeans

http://russelldavies.typepad.com/eggbaconchipsandbeans/

Quite possibly the antithesis of the food snob, Russell Davies visits cafes throughout the country always sampling one dish: eggs, bacon, chips and beans. With the knowledge of a fry-up expert, and some Welsh humour thrown in, this blog is a great resource if you're looking for your next greasy hit.

www.summersdale.com